D1186698

Archibald MacLeish
A Checklist

Archibald MacLeish

A Checklist

By Edward J. Mullaly
University of New Brunswick

The Kent State University Press

The Serif Series: Number 26
Bibliographies and Checklists
William White, General Editor
Wayne State University

A MAN'S WORK

An apple-tree, a cedar and an oak
Grow by the stone house in the rocky field
Where I write poems when my hand's in luck.
The cedar I put in: the rest are wild—

Wind dropped them. Apples strew the autumn ground
With black, sweet-smelling pips. The oak strews air,
Summers with shadow, winters with harsh sound.
The cedar's silent with its fruit to bear.

ARCHIBALD MACLEISH

Contents

Introduction

Archibald MacLeish's 'public' life, so far, spans a period of over fifty-five years. It includes undergraduate writing at Yale, service in the First World War, a law degree at Harvard, involvement in the American expatriate movement of the twenties, editorial writing for *Fortune*, some association with socialism in the early thirties, participation in the development of Roosevelt's New Deal, the leadership of the Library of Congress, governmental positions during the Second World War, the founding of UNESCO, active opposition to Senator Joseph McCarthy, acceptance of the Boylston professorship at Harvard, social comment during the active sixties, and more recently, the chance to speak for man on the occasion of the first moon landing. In the poem featured by the *New York Times* immediately following this event, MacLeish spoke of the earth as a "presence among us." His entire life has been devoted to an involved struggle with this presence in its personal, political, and social dimensions.

In the course of a very active life, MacLeish has created a large body of lyric poetry. At the same time, he has experimented with forms of verse drama for both radio and stage, and he has written, with less success, for television. MacLeish's prose extends from his articles for *The Yale Review* and *Fortune*, through his ideological defenses of democracy, to his most recent collection of essays, *A Continuing Journey*.

The publication of his collected poetry in 1952 brought him a
National Book Award, the Bollingen prize, and his second
Pulitzer prize. For his verse drama *J.B.*, seven years later,
MacLeish was awarded his third Pulitzer prize. Despite his
political involvement, and allowing for the rather superficial
nature of awards, the recognition given MacLeish should,
by the present day, have qualified him for that vague yet
significant eminence most recently held by Robert Frost.

Yet, from a critical standpoint, MacLeish has been all but
ignored. The one volume which analyzes his work has been
published as part of Twayne's United States Authors Series,
a series which includes not only the more recognized authors,
but also such figures as Bill Arp, F. Marion Crawford,
Vardis Fisher, Lafcadio Hearn, Petroleum V. Nasby, and
Albion W. Tourgee. The *PMLA* index for any given year in
this past decade has never listed more than three studies of
MacLeish's work. Thus it becomes apparent that, despite his
lasting contribution to American letters, and his close personal
involvement with other writers, MacLeish has received little
formal critical attention.

The present checklist forms an introduction to the MacLeish
canon as it stands in 1972. While it would be rash in the
extreme to assume that this volume lists all of MacLeish's
writings, it does contain a range of his ideas sufficiently wide
to indicate the directions in which his thoughts have travelled
during a long (and continuing) public life. Since the purpose
of a checklist is to make the reader simply aware of what
has been written, the list does not include the more exhaustive
documentation and description which would be required in
a formal bibliography. Information concerning British editions
of his works is included only when such volumes differ significantly from the American editions. Interviews and speeches
have appeared in such a wide range of publications that a
definitive listing of these must await future scholarship.

The annotated checklist of criticism also only indicates directions. Much of what has been said of MacLeish has been included in reviews of particular works. And while the list presented here does cover the whole spectrum of opinion, a student wishing to research the entire body of MacLeish criticism would have to examine as well the various periodical indices for the many reviews which have followed MacLeish's varied publications.

The present volume owes much to the MacLeish research which has gone before, particularly the Mizener bibliography published in 1938. From that time to the present various typed, stencilled, or printed listings have appeared. The present compilation combines these works with the results of personal research in order to bring this body of information together in a more readily accessible form.

The help of various hands in making this compilation must be acknowledged: St. Thomas University and The University of New Brunswick for research grants; The Harriet Irving Library Reference Department for its great patience and invaluable assistance; Professor George Healey for allowing use of the Cornell University Graduate Library; Anne Woods for research assistance; Professor Lauriat Lane, Jr., for scholarly guidance throughout the progress of this compilation; and May Mullaly for encouragement and constant aid in the many libraries through which we verified the material in this checklist.

E.J.M.

University of New Brunswick
August 1972

A Bibliographic Note

The most useful bibliographic work on MacLeish's writings
before the Second World War is Arthur Mizener's *Catalogue of
the First Editions of Archibald MacLeish* (New Haven:
Yale University Press, 1938). As well as giving information
on first editions, this catalog also contains listings of articles and
poems which had appeared in various periodicals. The Library
of Congress, Division of Bibliography, compiled an eighteen–
page supplement to Mizener in 1942 (collected by Florence
S. Hellman), which also included a short bibliography of
criticism. An eleven-leaf supplement to this was drawn up in
1944. In December 1944 the General Reference and Bibliography Division compiled a ten-leaf listing of MacLeish's
writings appearing in anthologies. In 1954 the same division
revised *Sixty American Poets, 1896–1944* selected by Allan
Tate, with a preliminary checklist by Francis Cheney, which
includes material on MacLeish (pp. 73–80). And, in 1968,
Victor Margolin compiled for the Library of Congress
a bibliography of more recent material, including translations,
records, and tapes, held by the Library and not included in
the earlier compilations.

Shorter bibliographies and checklists have appeared from
time to time. Frederic Melcher compiled a checklist for
Publishers Weekly, 124 (July 15, 1933) 180, which included
MacLeish's work up to *Poems, 1924–1933*. In 1939 Gerrish

Thurber compiled a bibliography of MacLeish books for the November 1 edition of the *Library Journal*.

In his *Bibliography of Bibliographies in American Literature* (New York: Bowker, 1970), Charles Nilon also lists other MacLeish bibliographies: Blank's *Merle Johnson's American First Editions* (Waltham, Mass.: Mark Press, 1965); Spiller and others, *Literary History of the United States* (New York: Macmillan, 1962); Woodress and others, *American Literary Scholarship* (Durham: Duke University Press, 1963 and following). Falk's *Archibald MacLeish* (New York: Twayne Publishers, 1965) gives much bibliographic information not only in its bibliography, but also in the many footnotes.

Information concerning individual reviews is to be found in periodical indices such as the *Reader's Guide to Periodical Literature*. The *PMLA* index and the *American Literature* listings supply information concerning scholarly articles on MacLeish, as do the two editions (1954 and 1970) of Lewis Leary's *Articles on American Literature* (Durham: Duke University Press).

I. Works by Archibald MacLeish

A. Books and pamphlets

1915

A1 *Class Poem 1915.* A leaflet distributed to the class-day audience on June 21, 1915. The poem was in four parts. Part I was later included in *Tower of Ivory* as "Baccalaureate" while parts II–IV were included in that volume as "Realities."

A2 *Yale University Prize Poem 1915: Songs For A Summer's Day.* New Haven: Yale University Press, 1915. 13pp. All sonnets of this sonnet sequence were later published in *Tower of Ivory*, with the exception of "Sarabande."

1917

A3 *Tower of Ivory.* New Haven: Yale University Press, 1917. xii, 71pp. Contains a foreword by Lawrence Mason.

1924

A4 *The Happy Marriage and Other Poems.* Boston and New York: Houghton Mifflin Company, 1924. ix, 80pp.

1925

A5 *The Pot of Earth.* Boston and New York: Houghton Mifflin Company, 1925. ix, 45pp.

1926

A6 *Nobodaddy*. Cambridge: Dunster House, 1926. 67pp. Foreword.

A7 *Streets in the Moon*. Boston and New York: Houghton Mifflin Company, 1926. xv, 102pp.

1928

A8 *The Hamlet of A. MacLeish*. Boston and New York: Houghton Mifflin Company, 1928. 45pp.

1929

A9 *Einstein*. Paris: Black Sun Press, 1929. [29pp.] This poem had previously been collected in *Streets in the Moon*.

1930

A10 *New Found Land*. Boston and New York: Houghton Mifflin Company, 1930. [v, 44pp.]

1932

A11 *Conquistador*. Boston and New York: Houghton Mifflin Company, 1932. 114pp.

A12 *Before March*. New York: Alfred A. Knopf, 1932. Published on October 15. A small chapbook containing the one poem, with drawings by Leja Gorska.

1933

A13 *Frescoes for Mr. Rockefeller's City*. New York: The John Day Company, 1933. 28pp. John Day Pamphlet no. 29.

A14 *Poems, 1924–1933*. Boston and New York: Houghton
Mifflin Company, 1933. viii, 304pp. Foreword.
First English Edition: *Poems*. London: Boriswood, 1935. The
edition does not contain "Conquistador."

1935

A15 *Panic*. Boston and New York: Houghton Mifflin
Company, 1935. x, 102pp. "A Note on the Verse."

1936

A16 *Public Speech*. New York: Farrar & Rinehart,
1936. ix, 30pp.

1937

A17 *The Fall of the City*. New York: Farrar & Rinehart
Inc., 1937. xiii, 33pp. Foreword.

1938

A18* *Christmas*. Boston? 1938. A composite sonnet; octave
by MacLeish and sestet by Theodore Spencer. A Christmas
card sent out by the Tavern Club in Boston to all
its members.

A19 *Air Raid*. New York: Harcourt, Brace and Company,
1938. vii, 36pp.

A20 *Land of the Free*. New York: Harcourt, Brace and
Company, 1938. 182pp.

1939

A21 *Libraries in the Contemporary Crisis*. An address
delivered at the Carnegie Institute, Pittsburgh, Pa., on

* Indicates works cited in articles or bibliographies or other sources
that I have not personally examined.

Founders' Day, October 19, 1939. Issued in booklet form
by the Library of Congress, November 1939.
Also published in the *Library Journal*, November 15, 1939.

A22 *America Was Promises*. New York: Duell, Sloan &
Pearce, 1939. 20pp.

1940

A23 Invitation from Librarian of Congress to attend the
opening of an exhibition of photographs by Miss Therese
Bonney, November 15, 1940. [typescript 2pp] This includes
an explanation of the exhibition of war photographs
by MacLeish.

A24 *The Irresponsibles*. New York: Duell, Sloan and Pearce,
1940. 34pp.
Also published in *Nation* 150 (May 18, 1940)
618–623 in a slightly different form.

1941

A25 *Lincoln in This Day*. Ottawa: 1941. An address delivered
before the Canadian Club of Ottawa, Canada,
February 12, 1941. Ottawa: 1941, issued by the Director
of Public Information. 8pp.

A26 *Declaration of Faith*. New York: The Council for
Democracy, 1941? [leaflet]

A27 *The Duty of Freedom*. Washington: Privately printed
for the United Typothetae of America, 1941. [8pp].

A28 *A Time to Speak*. Boston: Houghton Mifflin Co., 1941.
210pp.

A29 *The American Cause*. New York: Sloan and Pearce,
1941. 43pp. Foreword.

1942

A30 *Radio and War.* Washington: National Association
of Broadcasters, 1942? 7pp. An address to the 20th
annual convention, May 11, 1942.

A31 *American Opinion and the War.* Cambridge [England]:
The University Press, 1942. The Rede Lecture
delivered July 30, 1942.

1943

A32 *A Time to Act.* Boston: Houghton Mifflin Co., 1943.
198pp.

1944

A33 *The American Story.* New York: Sloan and Pearce,
1944. xii, 231pp. Foreword.

1948

A34 *Actfive and Other Poems.* New York: Random House,
1948. 63pp.

1950

A35 *Poetry and Opinion: the Pisan Cantos of Ezra Pound.*
Urbana, Ill.: University of Illinois Press, 1950. viii, 52pp.
Foreword. A lecture delivered at the University of
Illinois, 1950.

1951

A36 *Freedom is the Right to Choose.* Boston: Beacon Press,
1951. ix, 186pp. Foreword.

A37 *Poetry and the Belief in Man.* Charlottesville, Va.: 1951.
12pp. An address at the University of Virginia,
May 4, 1951. Stencilled.

1952

A38 *Collected Poems, 1917–1952*. Boston: Houghton Mifflin, 1952. viii, 407pp.

A39 *The Trojan Horse*. Boston: Houghton Mifflin, 1952. vii, 37pp. Publisher's Note by Paul Brooks.

1953

A40 *This Music Crept by Me Upon the Waters*. Cambridge: Harvard University Press, 1953. vii, 38pp. Foreword.
Also published in *Botteghe Oscure*, 11 (April 1953), 172–225 as "This Music Crept by Me on the Water."

1954

A41 *Songs for Eve*. Boston: Houghton Mifflin, 1954. vi, 58pp.

A42 *Art Education and the Creative Process*. New York, 1954. 11pp. Published for the Committee on Art Education by the Museum of Modern Art.
Reprinted as "Education and the Work of Art" in *A Continuing Journey*, pp. 234–241.

1958

A43 *Poetry and Journalism*. Minnesota Pamphlets, 1958. 21pp. Introduction by John W. Clark. Address given in Minneapolis, October 12, 1958.

A44 *J.B.* Boston: Houghton Mifflin, 1958. 153pp.
N.B. The Samuel French acting edition (New York, 1958) differs significantly from the Houghton Mifflin edition.

1959

A45 *Mr. Wilson and the Nation's Need*. New York: Woodrow Wilson Foundation, 1959.

1960

A46 *A Tribute by Archibald MacLeish on the Occasion of the 100th Anniversary Observance of the Birth of Jane Addams.* Chicago: Scott Foresman, 1960. 11pp.
Reprinted as "Jane Addams in Chicago" in *A Continuing Journey*, pp. 337–342.

1961

A47 *Poetry and Experience.* Boston: Houghton Mifflin, 1961. 204pp.

A48 *Three Short Plays.* New York: Dramatists Play Service, 1961. 86pp. Includes Notes on Production for "The Secret of Freedom." As well as *Air Raid* and *The Fall of the City*, this volume contains a television script entitled *The Secret of Freedom.*

1962

A49 *The Collected Poems of Archibald MacLeish.* Boston: Houghton Mifflin, 1962. xii, 417pp. Similar to *Collected Poems, 1917–1952*, it includes as well most of the poems from *Songs for Eve*. It omits *The Trojan Horse.*

1965

A50 *The Eleanor Roosevelt Story.* Boston: Houghton Mifflin, 1965. Text and illustrations from the motion picture.

A51 *Remarks of Mr. Archibald MacLeish on the Death of Justice Frankfurter, March 1, 1965.* Proceedings of the Bar and Officers of the Supreme Court of the United States. Washington: 1965. (offprint)

1967

A52 *An Evening's Journey to Conway Massachusetts.*
Northampton, Mass.: Gehenna Press, 1967. 21pp. An
outdoor play written for the bicentennial of the
town of Conway.

A53 *Herakles.* Boston: Houghton Mifflin, 1967. xi, 91pp.
Author's Note.

A54 *Remarks at the Dedication of the Wallace Library,
Fitchburh Massachusetts June 3rd 1967.* Worcester:
Achille J. St. Onge, 1967. 61pp. This miniature edition
also includes Emerson Greenway's "The Fitchburg Public
Library: A Brief History."

1968

A55 *A Continuing Journey.* Boston: Houghton Mifflin,
1968. x, 374pp.

A56 *The Wild Old Wicked Man and Other Poems.* Boston:
Houghton Mifflin, 1968. ix, 45pp.

1971

A57 *Scratch.* Boston: Houghton Mifflin, 1971. 116pp.

1972

A58 *The Human Season: Selected Poems 1926–1972.* Boston:
Houghton Mifflin, 1972. Foreword. 161pp.

B. Appearances of poetry and prose in books written or edited by others

1915

B1 *History of the Class of 1915*, ed. Albert H. Ely, Jr. New Haven: Yale University Press, 1915, 1930, 1952. (III Vols.)

Contains: "The Reed Player," "Sonnet" (I built an unnamed altar in my heart"), "Grief," "The Silence"—as well as one prose piece "The Cruise of the Domino," I, 441–444, 447–452; "Sophomore Year," I, 19–32; "Class Poem," II, 9–11; III, 11–13.

1919

B2 *The Yale Book of Student Verse 1910–1919*, ed. John Andrews and others. New Haven: Yale University Press, 1919. 212 pp.

Contains: "Class Poem," "The Reed Player," "Ballade," "The Altar," "Immortality," "Grief," "A Sampler," "My Body and I," "Imagery," "The Silence," "Lines to a Former Teacher at Yale: Musings of a Field Artillery Officer in France," pp. 151–169.

B3 *Kenneth: A Collection of Letters*. A volume concerning MacLeish's brother who was killed in the war. Edited and arranged by his mother. Chicago: privately printed, 1919. 131 pp.

Contains: "A Belgian Letter," "On a Memorial Stone," "The After-Spring," "To K. MacL," pp. 109–110, 120–124.

1926

B4 *American Criticism 1926*, ed. William A. Drake. New
   York: Brace and Company, 1926. xvii, 368 pp.
   Contains: "Santayana, the Poet," pp. 141–146.

1927

B5 *American Poetry 1927*; *A Miscellany*. New York:
   Harcourt, Brace And Company, 1927. 304 pp.
   Contains: "Bleheris," (which would be incorporated into Part III
   of the original version of *The Hamlet of A. MacLeish*,)
   "Revelation," "You, Andrew Marvell," "Weather," "Poem,"
   "Anniversary," pp. 225–237.

B6 *The American Caravan*, eds. Van Wyck Brooks and others.
   New York: The Macaulay Company, 1927. xv, 843 pp.
   Contains: "Fragment of a Biography" which, with a few changes,
   later became Section 4 of *The Hamlet of A. MacLeish*,
   pp. 374–376.

1929

B7 *American Poetry 1671–1928*, ed. Conrad Aiken. New York:
   The Modern Library, 1929. 362 pp.
   Contains: "L'An Trentiesme de Mon Age," "The Too-Late Born,"
   "Einstein," "You, Andrew Marvell," pp. 338–346.

1931

B8 *Living Authors*, ed. Dilly Tante. New York: The
   H. W. Wilson Company, 1931. vii, 466 pp.
   Contains: an autobiographical sketch, pp. 246–247.

1932

B9 *Housing America*, by the editors of *Fortune*. New York:
   Harcourt, Brace and Company, 1932. 159 pp.
   A reprint of MacLeish's *Fortune* articles on housing.

B10 *An Anthology of the Younger Poets*, ed. Oliver Wells.
Philadelphia: The Centaur Press, 1932. 184 pp.
Contains: a preface by MacLeish, "Nevertheless One Debt,"
IX–XIV.

1934

B11 *Permit Me Voyage*. James Agee. New Haven: Yale
University Press, 1934. 59 pp.
Contains: a foreword by MacLeish, pp. 5–7.

1935

B12 *What Is a Book?*, ed. Dale Warren. Boston: Houghton
Mifflin Company, 1935. 299 pp.
Contains: "Emotion and Form in Poetry," pp. 187–190, a
reprint from *The North American Review* where it was entitled
"Amy Lowell and the Art of Poetry." The sections dealing
with Amy Lowell are omitted.

1936

B13 *American Points of View, 1935*, ed. W. H. and K. C.
Cordell. Garden City: Doubleday, Doran & Company, 1936.
461 pp.
Contains: "The Writer and Revolution," pp. 357–361.

B14 *Jews in America*, by the editors of *Fortune*. New York:
Random House, 1936. 104 pp.
This is MacLeish's *Fortune* article of February, 1936.

B15 *Essay Annual*, collected by Erich A. Walter. Chicago:
Scott, Foresman and Company, 1936. 374 pp.
Contains: "A Stage for Poetry," pp. 169–175.

B16 *Portraits and Self-Portraits,* collected by Georges
Schreiber. Boston: x, 175 pp. Houghton Mifflin, 1936.
Contains: a short but interesting autobiographical note by
MacLeish, pp. 69–70.

1937

B17 *Background of War,* by the editors of *Fortune.* New York:
Alfred A. Knopf, 1937. 296 pp., index.
Contains: five articles by MacLeish. He did not write number iii,
"We Thank Our Fuhrer."

B18 *The Writer in a Changing World,* ed. Henry Hart.
New York: Equinox Cooperative Press, 1937. 256 pp.
Contains: "Spain and American Writers," pp. 56–62.

1938

B19 *New Directions in Prose and Poetry.* Norfolk, Conn.:
New Directions, 1938. (Volume III of this periodi-
cal, published annually.)
Contains: Notes on the soundtrack and picture form as used in
"Land of the Free," pp. 167–170.

1939

B20 *Law and Politics*; occasional papers of Felix Frankfurter,
1913–1938, ed. Archibald MacLeish and E. F. Prichard, Jr.
New York: Harcourt, Brace and Company, 1939.
xxiv, 352 pp.
Contains: a foreword by MacLeish, pp. ix–xxiv.

1940

B21 *A Tribute to A. Edward Newton.* U.S. Library of Congress.
Rare Book Division. Washington, Christmas, 1940.
[24 pp.]
Contains: a foreword, [p. 5].

1941

B22 *In Honor of a Man and an Ideal.* New York: The
Columbia Broadcasting System, 1941. 35 pp.
Contains: "A Superstition is Destroyed," a talk at a dinner in
honor of Edward R. Morrow, December 2, 1941, pp. 5–10.

B23 *The Free Company Presents,* compiled by James Boyd.
New York, 1941.
Contains: a radio play entitled "The States Talking," pp. 219–237.

B24 *Our Singing Country,* ed. J. A. Lomax and Alan Lomax.
New York: Macmillan, 1941. xxxiv, 416 pp.
Contains: an introduction, pp. vii–viii.

1942

B25 *An Interview with Archibald MacLeish,* by Robert Van
Gelder. New York: privately printed for the
Typophiles, 1942. 11 pp.
Contains: interview first published May 10, 1942, in the *New
York Times.*

B26 *A Free Man's Books,* address by MacLeish published
along with a letter by F. D. Roosevelt. Mount Vernon:
The Peter Pauper Press, 1942.
Contains: an address given May 16, 1942.

B27 *Fortress of Freedom.* Lucy Salamanca. Philadelphia:
J. B. Lippincott Co., 1942. 445 pp.
Contains: a foreword, pp. 9–11.

B28 *This Is My Best,* ed. Whit Burnett. New York:
Dial Press, 1942. xiv, 1180 pp.
Contains: comment on "America Was Promises," p. 123.

14

1944

B29 *Pioneers of Puerto Rico*. Muna Lee de Munoz Marin.
Boston: Heath, 1944. 80 pp.
Contains: a foreword, p. 1.

B30 *Love Letter from an Impossible Land*. William Meredith.
New Haven: Yale University Press, 1944, 50 pp.
Contains: a foreword, pp. 9–10.

1945

B31 *Books and Libraries in Wartime*, ed. Pierce Butler.
Chicago: University of Chicago Press, 1945. 159 pp.
Contains: "Library and the Nation," pp. 141–154.

B32 *Cut Is the Branch*. Charles E. Butler. New Haven:
Yale University Press, 1945. 61 pp.
Contains: a foreword, pp. 5–7.

1946

B33 *20 Non-Royalty One-Act Popular Classics*, ed. Margaret
Mayorga. New York: Greenberg, 1946. 458 pp.
Contains: "The States Talking," arranged as a choral chant,
pp. 441–458.

B34 *Family Circle*. Eve Merriam. New Haven: Yale University Press, 1946. 74 pp.
Contains: a foreword, pp. 5–7.

1947

B35 *American Authors Today*, ed. Whit Burnett and Charles
E. Slatkin. Boston: Ginn, 1947. xi, 559 pp.
Contains: a comment on "Colloquy for the States," p. 139.

1948

B36 *Last Chance*, ed. Clara Urquhart. Boston: Beacon Press, 1948. vii, 182 pp.

Contains: a general statement on world problems, pp. 33–39.

B37 *Ferment in Education*. Urbana: University of Illinois Press, 1948. 223 pp.

Contains: "The Terrible Responsibility of the Teacher," pp. 41–49.

1949

B38 *Martha Hillard MacLeish*. Martha Hillard MacLeish. Conway, Mass.: privately printed, 1949.

Contains: a foreword, pp. vii–xxxii.

1951

B39 Roosevelt Day dinner address, in James E. Murray, Extension of remarks in the Senate of the United States, January 29, 1951. Congressional Record, 82nd Congress, 2nd session, v. 97: A416–418.

Contains: an address at the Roosevelt Day dinner, held under the auspices of Americans for Democratic Action, Washington, D. C., January 26, 1951.

B40 *Modern Poetry, American and British*, ed. K. Friar and J. M. Brinnin. New York: Appleton Century-Crofts, 1951. xviii, 580 pp.

Contains: comment on "Einstein," p. 521.

1954

B41 *Literature in the Modern World*, lectures delivered at George Peabody College for Teachers, 1951–1954. Nashville: Bureau of Publications, George Peabody College for Teachers, 1954. 144 pp.

Contains: a lecture "The Reading and Teaching of Modern Poetry," given July 28, 1952, pp. 17–29.

B42 *The Last of the Bohemians*. A. Beucler. New York:
W. Sloan Associates, 1954. xii, 237 pp.
Contains: an introduction, pp. vii–xii.

1955

B43 *The Unity of Knowledge*, ed. L. G. Leary. Garden City:
Doubleday, 1955. xiv, 306 pp.
Contains: "The Language of Poetry," a paper prepared for the
fifth Columbia University Bicentennial Conference, October 1954,
pp. 215–230.

1960

B44 The Arts and Sciences and the National Purpose, in
John V. Lindsay, Extension of remarks in the House of
Representatives, May 11, 1961. Congressional Record,
87th Congress, 1st session, V. 107: A3962–A3963.
Contains: an address delivered at the Yale University
convocation of alumni organization, October 1960.

B45 *Emily Dickinson: Three Views*. Amherst: Amherst College
Press, 1960. 46 pp.
Contains: "The Private World," pp. 13–26.

B46 *The First Freedom*. R. B. Downs. The American Library
Association, 1960. xiii, 469 pp.
Contains: "A Tower Which Will Not Yield," pp. 323–329.

B47* *The Wordless Flesh*. Gerald P. Fitzgerald. Cambridge,
1960.
Contains: a foreword.

1961

B48 *Art and the Craftsman*, ed. J. Harned and Neil Goodman.
New Haven, 1961. 352 pp.
Contains: "The Limits of Creative Writing Courses," pp. 280–282.

B49 *Majesty and Mischief*; a mixed tribute to F.D.R.
William S. White. New York: McGraw-Hill, 1961. 221 pp.
Contains: the Official White House announcement of President
Roosevelt's death, p. 33.

1962

B50 *Let Freedom Ring*, by the editors of *American Heritage*.
New York: American Heritage Publishing Co., 1962. 64 pp.
Contains: "The American Bell," the text of a sound and light
spectacular presented at Independence Hall in Philadelphia
concerned with the Liberty Bell and the events leading to the
signing of the Declaration of Independence, pp. 49–59.

B51 *The Estate of Poetry*. Edwin Muir. Cambridge:
Harvard University Press, 1962. 118 pp.
Contains: "A Memoir of Muir," a foreword later published in
A Continuing Journey, pp. vii–xviii.

1963

B52 *Addresses Delivered at the Center for Hellenic Studies*.
Harvard University Press, 1963. 46 pp.
Contains: "An Hellenic Center in Washington," later published
in *A Continuing Journey*, pp. 37–47.

1964

B53 *The Dialogues of Archibald MacLeish and Mark Van
Doren*, ed. W. V. Bush. New York: Dutton, 1964. 285 pp.
Contains: the dialogues, along with some bibliographic
references.

1967

B54 *Think Back on Us*. Malcolm Cowley. Carbondale:
Southern Illinois University Press, 1967. xv, 400 pp.
Contains: MacLeish vs. Cowley: "Lines for an Interment,"
pp. 35–39.

C. Poems first appearing in periodicals and newspapers

1911

C1 "Gifts," *Yale Literary Magazine*, 77 (October 1911), 26.

1912

C2 "Song of the Slave," *Yale Literary Magazine*, 77 (April 1912), 262.

C3 "The Marshes," *Yale Literary Magazine*, 78 (December 1912), 95.

1913

C4 "Wanderlust," *Yale Literary Magazine*, 78 (April 1913), 281.

C5 "The Silence," *Yale Literary Magazine*, 78 (April 1913), 299. Reprinted in *Songs for a Summer's Day*, 12.

C6 "The Reed Player," *Yale Literary Magazine*, 78 (May 1913), 3. Anthologized in *History of the Class of 1915*. Reprinted in *Tower of Ivory*, 65.

C7 "The Many Dead," *Yale Literary Magazine*, 78 (June 1913), 402.

C8 "Ballade," *Yale Literary Magazine*, 79 (November 1913), 55. Reprinted in *Tower of Ivory*, 49.

1914

C9 "Sonnet," *Yale Literary Magazine*, 79 (May 1914), 363.
Reprinted as "The Altar," in *Songs for a Summer's Day*, p. 5.

1915

C10 "Grief," *Yale Review*, 4 (April 1915), 576–577.
Anthologized in *History of the Class of 1915*. Reprinted in *Tower of Ivory*, 22.

C11 "The Grail," *Yale Literary Magazine*, 80 (June 1915), 401–402.

1916

C12 "Echo," *Harper's Weekly*, 62 (April 29, 1916), 464.
Reprinted in *Tower of Ivory*, 22.

1919

C13 "On a Memorial Stone," *Lyric*, April 1919.
Anthologized in *Kenneth: A Collection of Letters*.

1920

C14 "A Belgian Letter," "Invocation," "L'Amour de moi," "Consolation," *Parabalou*, no. 1, issued by the Publisher From Will Warren's Den, Farmington, Conn., 1920, pp. 5–9.

C15 "Chambers of Imagery," "Creation," "Sonnet" ("O too dull brain, O unperceiving nerves"), "Sonnet" ("From epic metaphor, poetic phrase"), "Sonnet" ("It is not tragical that love should die"), "Two Sestets," "The Tomb of the Abbess of Tours," *Parabalou*, no. 2, 1920, pp. 27–30.

1921

C16 "Hunters," "Kenneth," "Hypocrites," "Bronze," "Alien,"
"For Remembrance," "Omniscience," *Parabalou,*
no. 3, 1921, pp. 3–7.

1922

C17 'The Lord Chancellor Prepares His Opinion," *North
American Review,* 216 (August 1922), 209–211.
Reprinted in *The Happy Marriage and Other Poems,* 40.

1923

C18 "Hands," *Atlantic,* 131 (May 1923), 643. Reprinted in
The Happy Marriage and Other Poems, 47.

C19 "High Road," *New Republic,* 34 (May 16, 1923), 323.

C20 "Impulse," *New Republic,* 36 (August 29, 1923), 12.

C21 "Separate," *Atlantic,* 132 (November 1923), 628.

C22 "Years Ago," *Atlantic,* 132 (December 1923), 758–759.
Reprinted in *The Happy Marriage and Other Poems,* 76.

1924

C23 "Captured," *Yale Review,* 13 (January 1924), 346.

C24 "The Farm," *Atlantic,* 133 (April 1924), 483.
Reprinted in *Streets in the Moon,* 72.

C25 "Chiaroscuro," "Take Arms of Irony," *North American
Review,* 219 (May 1924), 640. "Chiaroscuro" was
reprinted in *Streets in the Moon,* 69.

C26 "Corporate Entity," *New Republic,* 39 (July 2, 1924)
160. Reprinted in *Streets in the Moon,* 94.

C27 "Selene Afterwards," *Atlantic*, 134 (August 1924), 215–216. Reprinted in *Streets in the Moon*, 29.

C28 "But There Are Times," "Beauty," *Current Opinion*, 77 (August 1924), 225.

C29 "The Tea Party," *Atlantic*, 134 (September 1924), 375. Reprinted in *Streets in the Moon*, 67.

C30 "Cathedral," *North American Review*, 220 (September 1924), 156.

C31 "Columnist," *The New Republic*, 40 (October 29, 1924), 226. Reprinted in *Streets in the Moon*, 95.

1925

C32 "Epitaph for a Sea Grave," *Independent*, 114 (April 11, 1925), 411.

C33 "The End of the World," *New Republic*, 42 (May 20, 1925), 342. Reprinted in *Streets in the Moon*, 101.

C34 "Conversation Balnéaire," *Atlantic*, 136 (July 1925), 97. Reprinted in *Streets in the Moon*, 75.

C35 "Toward a Romantic Revival," *New Republic*, 44 (September 16, 1925), 99.

C36 "Train-stop: Night," "Pastoral," *Commerce*, 5 (Automne 1925), 128–130. Reprinted in *Streets in the Moon*, 15, 35.

C37 "Signature for Tempo," "Memorial Rain," *Yale Review*, 15 (October 1925), 55–58. Reprinted in *Streets in the Moon*, 9, 54.

C38 "Question in Time of Eternity," *North American Review*, 222 (December 1925), 286. Reprinted in *Streets in the Moon*, 91.

C39 "Chartres," "Voyage in Provence," *Voices*, 5 (December 1925), 91. Reprinted in *Streets in the Moon*, 22, 85.

1926

C40 "For Amy Lowell," *Atlantic*, 137 (January 1926), 46.

C41 "Salle d'Attente," *Independent*, 116 (February 20, 1926), 218. Reprinted in *Streets in the Moon*, 15.

C42 "No Lamp Has Ever," *Criterion*, 4 (April 1926), 312.

C43 "Memories of A–," *Nation*, 122 (June 16, 1926), 671.

C44 "Ars Poetica," *Poetry*, 28 (June 1926), 126–127. Reprinted in *Streets in the Moon*, 37.

C45 "In My Thirtieth Year," *Saturday Review of Literature*, 2 (July 3, 1926), 897. Reprinted in *Streets in the Moon*, 13.

C46 "Nocturne," *Dial*, 81 (July 1926), 65. Reprinted in *Streets in the Moon*, 20.

1927

C47 "Signature Anonyme," *transition*, 1 (April 1927), 124–125. Reprinted in *New Found Land*.

C48 "Return," "Gobi," *Commerce*, 12 (Eté 1927), 44–50. "Return" was reprinted in *New Found Land*.

C49 "Land's End," *Criterion*, 6 (July 1927), 14. Reprinted in *New Found Land*.

1928

C50 "O Sun, Instigator of Cocks," *Dial*, 84 (May 1928), 376. Reprinted as "Poem Dedicatory" in *New Found Land*.

C51 "And Forty-second Street," *transition*, 13 (Summer 1928), 42–43. Reprinted in *New Found Land*.

C52 "Il Ne Reste Que Vos Photos," *Saturday Review of Literature*, 5 (October 20, 1928), 265. Reprinted in *Poems, 1924–1933*, 55, as "De Votre Bonheur Il Ne Reste Que Vos Photos."

C53 "Reproach to Dead Poets," *Yale Review*, 18 (December 1928), 345–346. Reprinted in *New Found Land*.

1929

C54 ". . . memory green," *New Republic*, 57 (January 9, 1929), 210. Reprinted in *New Found Land*.

C55 "American Letter," *Bookman*, 68 (January 1929), 509–511. Reprinted in *New Found Land*.

C56 "Unanswered Letter to a Lady Novelist," "Epistle to the Rapalloan," "Communication to Léon-Paul Fargue," *Poetry* 33 (January 1929), 184–187. "Communication to Léon-Paul Fargue" reprinted in *Poems, 1924–1933*, 141, as "Epistle to Léon-Paul Fargue."

C57 "Sentiments for a Dedication," *Nation*, 128 (February 13, 1929), 194. Reprinted in *Poems, 1924–1933*, 76.

C58 "Tourist Death," *transition*, 15 (February 1929), 37. Reprinted in *New Found Land*.

C59 "Sonnet on First Looking into the American Novel," *New Republic*, 58 (March 13, 1929), 96.

C60 "History of the World," *New Republic*, 58 (April 24, 1929), 278.

C61 "Aeterna Poetae Memoria," *Saturday Review of Literature*, 5 (May 11, 1929), 993. Reprinted in *Poems, 1924–1933*, 91.

C62 "October 14, 1928, For K. MacL.," *Nation*, 128 (May 22, 1929), 614.

C63 "Lady A'h A'h," *New Republic*, 59 (June 5, 1929), 72.

C64 "Men," *New Republic*, 59 (June 26, 1929), 144.
Reprinted in *New Found Land*.

C65 "To Praisers of Women," *Harpers*, 159 (September
1929), 485.

C66 "Immortal Autumn," *Yale Review*, 19 (September
1929), 26. Reprinted in *New Found Land*.

C67 "Conquistador," *Yale Review*, 19 (December 1929),
233–243. Díaz' Preface to the long poem. [A comparison
of this with the finalized version offers an excellent
opportunity to discover those areas in which the poet
was concerned in making his final revisions.]

1930

C68 "Cartoon," *New Republic*, 61 (February 12, 1930), 321.
Revised as "Contemporary Portrait" in *"The Wild Old
Wicked Man" and other Poems*, p. 37.

C69 "Epistle to be Left in the Earth," *New Republic*, 62
(April 30, 1930), 291. Reprinted in *Poems,
1924–1933*, 159.

C70 "Cinema of a Man/In Memoriam: Harry Crosby,"
Transition, 19–20 (June 1930), 230–231.
Reprinted in *New Found Land*.

1932

C71 "Invocation to the Social Muse," *New Republic*, 72
(October 26, 1932), 296. Reprinted in *Poems,
1924–1933*, 166–168.

1933

C72 "Unfinished History," *New Yorker*, (January 21, 1933),
16. Reprinted in *Poems, 1924–1933*, 50.

C73 "1933," *Yale Review*, 22 (June 1933), 649–655.
Reprinted in *Poems, 1924–1933*. This poem was reprinted
as "Elpenor" in *Collected Poems 1917–1952*, but as
"1933" in *Collected Poems* (1962). [Both of these later
editions contain a significantly shortened version of
the poem.]

C74 "Men of My Century Loved Mozart," *New Republic*,
77 (December 13, 1933), 132. Reprinted in *Poems*,
1924–1933, 89.

C75 Excerpt from *Panic*, *Nation*, 140 (March 6, 1935), 281.

1935

C76 Selections from *Panic*, *New Theatre*, (March 1935), 10-12.

C77 "The German Girls! The German Girls!," *New Masses*,
17 (December 17, 1935), 23. Reprinted in *Public Speech*.

1936

C78 "Pole Star for This Year," *New Republic*, 85 (January 1,
1936), 224. Reprinted in *Public Speech*.

C79 "The Lost Speakers," *Saturday Review of Literature*,
13 (February 8, 1936), 6. Reprinted in *Public Speech*.

C80 "Speech to Those Who Say Comrade," *New Masses*,
18 (February 11, 1936), 13. Reprinted in *Public Speech*.

C81 "Speech to the Detractors," *Nation*, 142 (March 4,
1936). Reprinted in *Public Speech*.

1937

C82 "Speech to Scholars," *Saturday Review of Literature,* 16 (June 12, 1937), 12.

1939

C83 "Colloquy for the States," *Atlantic,* 164 (October 1939), 484–487. Reprinted in *A Time to Act,* 1–6.

C84 "America Was Promises," *New Republic,* 101 (November 8, 1939), 46–48.

1940

C85 "Discovery of This Time," *Poetry,* 57 (October 1940), 1–3.

1941

C86 "The Western Sky," *Free World,* 1 (October 1941) 1. Reprinted in *A Time To Act,* 195–198.

1944

C87 "Young Dead Soldiers," *Free World,* 7 (January 1944), 7. Reprinted in *Actfive and Other Poems,* 60.

1946

C88 "Brave New World," *Atlantic,* 178 (September 1946), 36–37. Reprinted in *Actfive and Other Poems,* 61.

1947

C89 "What Must," *Atlantic,* 179 (January 1947), 55–56. Reprinted in *Actfive and Other Poems,* 46.

1949

C90 "The Grave at Hyde Park," *Atlantic,* 183 (January 1949), 59.

C90 "The Black Day," *New Republic*, 120 (January 10, 1949), 7.

1950

C92 "Slow March for the Holy War," *Nation*, 171 (December 16, 1950), 597.

1951

C93 "The Renovated Temple," *Atlantic*, 188 (December 1951), 42. Reprinted in *Collected Poems 1917–1952*, 168.

1952

C94 "The Burial," *Atlantic*, 189 (February 1952), 57. Reprinted in *Collected Poems 1917–1952*, 155.

C95 "Old Men in the Leaf Smoke," "Where the Hayfields Were," "What the Old Women Say," "The Patriots," "The Bed," "They Come no More, Those Words, Those Finches," *Atlantic*, 189 (June 1952), 40–41. All reprinted except "The Patriots," in *Collected Poems 1917–1952*, 152, 153, 158, 155, 151.

C96 "What Riddle Asked the Sphinx," *Atlantic*, 190 (October 1952), 69. Reprinted in *Collected Poems 1917–1952*, 156.

C97 "Hypocrite Auteur," *Poetry*, 81 (October 1952), 41–45. Reprinted in *Collected Poems 1917–1952*, 173.

C98 "Poet," "The Wood Dove at Sandy Spring," "And Out of Weakness, Song," "With Age Wisdom," "My Naked Aunt," "St. Philip's Church in Antigua," *Atlantic*, 194 (July 1954), 42–43. All except "And Out of Weakness, Song," reprinted in *Songs For Eve*, 51, 45, 42, 50, 46.

1955

C99 "Sweet Land of Liberty," *Collier's*, 136 (July 8, 1955), 44–55.

1956

C100 "Poem for a Festival of Art at the Boston Public Gardens," *Saturday Review*, 39 (July 28, 1956), 11. [According to John Ciardi in *Saturday Review* (September 1, p. 23), this poem was intended to be without a title, and the first two lines were used as the title by mistake.]

1958

C101 "A View of the Lime Quarry on the Slopes of Sermoneta from the Hill Above the River Ninfa," *Botteghe Oscure* 21 (1958), 181–182. Revised for *"The Wild Old Wicked Man" and Other Poems*, 35.

1960

C102 "Brooks Atkinson," *Equity*, 45 (September 1960), 4. Reprinted in *"The Wild Old Wicked Man" And Other Poems*, 32.

C103 "Celestial Politics," *Nation*, 191 (December 31, 1960), 527.

1961

C104 "The Gunshot; E. H.," *Atlantic*, 208 (November 1961), 46. Reprinted as "Hemingway" in *"The Wild Old Wicked Man" And Other Poems*, 28.

1962

C105 "At the Lincoln Memorial," *New York Times*, September 22, 1962, p. 12. Reprinted in *Collected Poems of Archibald MacLeish*, 198.

1966

C106 "Sunset," *Yale Literary Magazine,* 135 (September 1966), 45. Reprinted as "Cummings" in *"The Wild Old Wicked Man" And Other Poems,* 27.

1967

C107 "Where a Poet's From," *Saturday Review,* 50 (December 2, 1967), 21. Reprinted in *"The Wild Old Wicked Man" And Other Poems,* 25.

1968

C108 "The Boatmen of Santorin," Program for the library dedication exercises at the University of Utah, May 17, 1968. Reprinted in *"The Wild Old Wicked Man" And Other Poems,* 4.

C109 "The Wild Old Wicked Man," "Hurricane," "Waking," "Black Humor," "Boy in the Roman Zoo," *Saturday Review,* 51 (August 10, 1968), 25. Reprinted in *"The Wild Old Wicked Man" And Other Poems,* 44, 1, 6, 9, 10.

C110 "Observations of P. Ovidius Naso on the Incidence of Sex in the Contemporary Novel," *Harper's,* 237 (August 1968), 68. Reprinted in *"The Wild Old Wicked Man" And Other Poems,* 21

1969

C111 "Voyage to the Moon," *New York Times,* July 21, 1969, p. 1.

1970

C112 "State Funeral," *Atlantic,* 225 (April 1970), 63.

C113 "In and Come In," *The Quarterly Journal of the Library of Congress,* 27 (April 1970), 132.

C114 "Thrush on the Island of Bara," *The National Geographic*, 137 (May 1970), 692–693.

1972
C115 Untitled ["This Year's Bees Are Loved in Last Year's Flowers."] *New York Times*, May 4, 1972, p. 45.

D. Prose first appearing in periodicals and newspapers

The Fortune *articles listed here were all written by MacLeish although, according to Mizener's 1938 bibliography, "material for them was not always gathered by him alone."*

1912

D1 "On Bells," *Yale Literary Magazine*, 77 (May 1912), 299–302.

D2 "Hedgerow and Stonewall," *Yale Literary Magazine*, 77 (June 1912), 349–352.

D3 "The Shears of Atropos," *Yale Literary Magazine*, 78 (October 1912), 14–20. [One of the few short stories written by MacLeish while he was an undergraduate.]

1913

D4 "The Charity of Love," *Yale Literary Magazine*, 78 (March 1913), 253–260. Short Story.

D5 "The Gypsy Winds," *Yale Literary Magazine*, 78 (March 1913), 264–267.

D6 "Laus Veneris," *Yale Literary Magazine*, 78 (April 1913), 292–298. Short Story.

D7 "The Virtues of Vice," *Yale Literary Magazine*, 78 (May 1913), 352–359. Short Story.

D8 "The Mystery of Change," *Yale Literary Magazine*, 78 (May 1913), 367–370.

D9 "The Roads of Riga Mountain," *Yale Literary Magazine*, 78 (June 1913), 403–409. Short Story.

D10 "The Age of Chivalry," *Yale Literary Magazine*, 79 (November 1913), 71–75. Short Story.

1914

D11 "The Man Who Played God," *Yale Literary Magazine*, 79 (January 1914), 159–166. Short Story.

D12 "The Cruise of the Domino," *Yale Literary Magazine*, 79 (February 1914), 213–218.

D13 "To the Patient Few," *Yale Literary Magazine*, 79 (April 1914), 283–286.

1915

D14 "For Reformers Only," *Yale Literary Magazine*, 80 (March 1915), 281–284.

1921

D15 "Professional Schools of Liberal Education," *Yale Review*, 10 (January 1921), 362–372.

1923

D16 "The New Age and the New Writers," *Yale Review*, 12 (January 1923), 314–321.

D17 "The Next Philosophy," *North American Review*, 217 (May 1923), 698–704. [This article, written with Lawrence Mason, purported to be a review of *The Lyric Tense*, by Peter Sczornik. MacLeish later admitted (*Poetry*, 73 (October 1948), 40) that both the book and its author were fictitious.]

D18 "Black Armour," *New Republic*, 37 (December 5, 1923), Pt. II, 16.

1924

D19 "The Beginning of Things," *North American Review*, 219 (March 1924), 367–371.

1925

D20 "Amy Lowell and the Art of Poetry," *North American Review*, 221 (March 1925), 508–521.

D21 "Four Poets," *Yale Review*, 14 (April 1925), 587–592.

D22 "Santayana the Poet," *Bookman* [New York], 62 (October 1925), 187–189.

1928

D23 "Behold the Critiquins," *Saturday Review of Literature*, 4 (January 21, 1928), 529–531.

1929

D24 "A New Life of Melville," *Bookman* [New York], 69 (April 1929), 183–185.

D25 "An Anonymous Generation," *Saturday Review of Literature*, 6 (December 7, 1929), 503–504. Reprinted in *A Time to Speak*, pp. 152–158.

1930

D26 "Pie," *Fortune*, 1 (March 1930), 91ff.

D27 "Gold," *Fortune*, 1 (May 1930), 39ff.

D28 "New York Times," *Fortune*, 1 (May 1930), 56ff.

D29 "Albert Henry Wiggin," *Fortune*, 1 (June 1930), 90ff.

D30 "Man-made Immortals," *Fortune*, 1 (June 1930), 66ff.

D31 "Skyscrapers, I," *Fortune*, 2 (July 1930), 33ff.

D32 "Skyscrapers, II," *Fortune*, 2 (August 1930), 60ff.

D33 "Alfred Emanuel Smith," *Fortune*, 2 (September 1930), 52ff.

D34 "Skyscrapers, III," *Fortune* 2 (September 1930), 54ff.

D35 "Persian Rugs," *Fortune*, 2 (October 1930), 46ff.

D36 "Skyscrapers, IV," *Fortune*, 2 (October 1930), 85ff.

D37 "Rentschlers," *Fortune*, 2 (November 1930), 73ff.

D38 "Skyscrapers, V," *Fortune*, 2 (November 1930), 77ff.

D39 "Armored Cars," *Fortune*, 2 (December 1930), 46ff.

D40 "Skyscrapers, VI," *Fortune*, 2 (December 1930), 84ff.

1931

D41 "Corporation Lawyers," *Fortune*, 3 (January 1931), 61ff.

D42 "Uniforms," *Fortune*, 3 (January 1931), 74ff.

D43 "Harrimans," *Fortune*, 3 (June 1931), 80ff.

D44 "Nevertheless One Debt," *Poetry*, 88 (July 1931), 208–216. Reprinted in *A Time to Speak*, pp. 52–58.

D45 "Labor," *Fortune*, 4 (August 1931), 54ff.

D46 "Samuel Insull II," *Fortune*, 4 (September 1931), 74ff.

D47 "Depression of '93–'97," *Fortune*, 4 (December 1931), 78ff.

1932

D48 "To the Young Men of Wall Street," *Saturday Review of Literature*, 8 (January 16, 1932), 453–454.

D49 "Eugene Meyer," *Fortune*, 5 (January 1932), 28ff.

D50 "Housing, I," *Fortune*, 5 (February 1932), 61ff.

D51 "Rivera Fresco," *Fortune*, 5 (February 1932), 40ff.

D52 "Housing, II," *Fortune*, 5 (March 1932), 44ff.

D53 "Secretary of State," *Fortune*, 5 (March 1932), 37ff.

D54 "Housing, III," *Fortune*, 5 (April 1932), 34ff.

D55 "Housing, IV," *Fortune*, 5 (May 1932), 67ff.

D56 "Fourteenth Amendment," *Fortune*, 5 (June 1932), 52ff.

D57 "Housing, V," *Fortune*, 5 (June 1932), 67ff.

D58 "Bullfighting," *Fortune*, 6 (July 1932), 70ff.

D59 "Housing, VI," *Fortune*, 6 (July 1932), 60ff.

D60 "Hoover's Fortune," *Fortune*, 6 (August 1932), 32ff.

D61 "More Housing," *Fortune*, 6 (August 1932), 94ff.

D62 "Housing," *Fortune*, 6 (September 1932), 74ff.

D63 "Unemployment Relief," *Fortune*, 6 (September 1932), 18ff.

D64 "Hogs," *Fortune*, 6 (October 1932), 38ff.

D65 "Housing," *Fortune*, 6 (October 1932), 76ff.

D66 "Social Cant," *New Republic*, 73 (December 21, 1932), 156–158.

D67 "Labor Saving Machines," *Fortune*, 6 (December 1932), 24ff.

1933

D68 "Technocracy," *Saturday Review of Literature*, 9 (January 14, 1933), 373–374.

D103 "The Writer and Revolution," *Saturday Review of Literature*, 11 (January 26, 1935), 441–442.

D104 "Taxation," *Fortune*, 11 (January 1935), 41ff.

D105 "Marriner Stoddard Eccles," *Fortune*, 11 (February 1935), 62–65.

D106 "United States Senate," *Fortune*, 11 (February 1935), 46ff.

D107 "An Interview with Archibald MacLeish," *Daily Worker*, March 15, 1935, p. 5.

D108 "Social Security," *Fortune*, 11 (March 1935), 52ff.

D109 "Soviet Art," *Fortune*, 11 (March 1935), 62ff.

D110 "The Democratic Party," *Fortune*, 11 (April 1935), 62ff.

D111 "George V," *Fortune*, 11 (June 1935), 54ff.

D112 "Cotton," *Fortune*, 12 (July 1935), 34ff.

D113 "Words to be Spoken," *New Republic*, 84 (August 28, 1935), 73.

D114 "Chrysler," *Fortune*, 12 (August 1935), 30ff.

D115 "Fortune Award," *Fortune*, 12 (August 1935), 57ff.

D116 "Women in Business, II," *Fortune*, 12 (August 1935), 50ff.

D117 "Women in Business, III," *Fortune*, 12 (September 1935), 81ff.

D118 "A Stage for Poetry," *Stage*, 13 (November 1935), 38–39. Reprinted in *A Time to Speak*, pp. 74–80.

D119 "Grasslands," *Fortune*, 12 (November 1935), 59ff.
A section from this was published as "Green River"
in *A Time to Speak*, pp. 176–184.

D120 "Roosevelt," *Fortune*, 12 (December 1935), 102ff.

1936

D121 "Starvation Amidst Plenty," *Stage*, 13 (January
1936), 31–32.

D122 "Felix Frankfurter," *Fortune*, 13 (January 1936), 63ff.

D123 "Jews in America," *Fortune*, 13 (February 1936), 79ff.

D124 "Agriculture," *Fortune*, 13 (March 1936), 80ff.

D125 "Department of Agriculture," *Fortune*, 13 (April
1936), 95ff.

D126 "Gorki the Artisan," *New Masses*, 20 (August 4,
1936), 12–13.

D127 "The Tradition of the People," *New Masses*, 20
(September 1, 1936), 25–27. Reprinted as "Mr. Sandburg
and the Doctrinaires" in *A Time to Speak*, pp. 36–41.

D128 "The Farmer Does Without," *Fortune*, 14 (September
1936), 87ff. [A shorter version appears as "Landscape
of a People" in *A Time to Speak*, pp. 185–190.]

D129 "Of Many Men on Little Land," *Fortune*, 14 (September 1936), 92. Reprinted in *A Time To Speak*,
pp. 190–192.

D130 "Fortune Quarterly Survey," *Fortune*, 14 (December
1936), a 4-page insert.

D131 "UNESCO'S Task," *American Association of
University Professors Bulletin*, 32 (December 1936),
605–609.

40

1937

D132 "Joseph Taylor Robinson," *Fortune*, 15 (January 1937), 88ff.

D133 "Political Realignment," *Fortune*, 15 (February 1937), 67ff.

D134 "Background of War—British Foreign Policy," *Fortune*, 15 (March 1937), 97ff.

D135 "Background of War—The Struggle in Spain," *Fortune*, 15 (April 1937), 81ff.

D136 "Unemployed Arts," *Fortune*, 15 (May 1937), 109ff.

D137 "The War Is Ours," *New Masses*, 23 (June 22, 1937), 5–6.

D138 "Background of War—Le Front Populaire," *Fortune*, 15 (June 1937), 82ff.

D139 "Index of American Design," *Fortune*, 15 (June 1937), 103ff.

D140 "Background of War—Who Dares to Fight," *Fortune*, 16 (July 1937), 69ff.

D141 "Background of War—The Bear That Shoots Like a Man," *Fortune*, 16 (August 1937), 70ff.
D142 "The American Ides of March," *Nation*, 145 (December 4, 1937), 617.

D143 "South America," *Fortune*, 16 (December 1937), 92ff.

1938

D144 "Federal Taxes," *Fortune*, 17 (January 1938), 46.

D145 "Public Speech and Private Speech in Poetry,"
Yale Review, 27 (March 3, 1938), 536–547. Reprinted
in *A Time to Speak*, pp. 59–69.

D146 "In Challenge Not Defense," *Poetry*, 52 (July,
September 1938), 212–219, 342–343. Reprinted in *A
Time to Speak*, pp. 1–7.

D147 "Thucydides in Prague," *Nation*, 147 (October 8,
1938), 354–355.

D148 "Munich and the Americans," *Nation*, 147
(October 15, 1938), 370–371.

D149 "Exploring in Drama," *New York Times*,
October 30, 1938, p. 12.

1939

D150 "Propaganda vs. Hollywood," *Stage*, 16 (January
1939), 11–12.

D151 "Dry Tortugas," *Vogue*, 93 (February 1, 1939),
69, 159.

D152 "Freedom to End Freedom," *Survey Graphic*, 28
(February 1939), 117–119. Reprinted in *A Time To
Speak*, pp. 131–139.

D153 "How Big Business Can Make Friends," *New Republic*,
98 (March 22, 1939), 187–188.

D154 "Liberalism and The Anti-fascist Front," *Survey
Graphic*, 28 (May 1939), 321–323. Reprinted as "The
Affirmation" in *A Time to Speak*, pp. 8–16.

D155 "The Young Can Choose; Democracy's Only Defense
Is a Good Attack," *Common Sense*, 8 (May 1939), 13–14.

D156 "Letter to Mr. Angleton," *Furioso* [a magazine of verse], 1 (Summer 1939), 1–2.

D157 "Poetry and the Public World," *Atlantic*, 163 (June 1939), 823–830. Reprinted in *A Time to Speak*, pp. 81–96.

D158 "Let Us All Cooperate," *Library Journal*, 64 (August 1939), 570.

D159 "Libraries in the Contemporary Crisis," *Library Journal*, 64 (November 15, 1939), 879–882.

D160 "Youth Speaks on Religion in Democracy," *McCalls*, 67 (December 1939), 14ff.

1940

D161 "The Art of the Good Neighbour," *Nation*, 140 (February 10, 1940), 170–172. Reprinted in *A Time to Speak*, pp. 199–205.

D162 "Mr. Justice Frankfurter," *Life*, 8 (February 12, 1940), 53–56. Reprinted as "Portrait of a Living Man" in *A Time to Speak*, pp. 165–175.

D163 "War Is Ours; abstract," *Saturday Evening Post*, 212 (February 17, 1940), 91.

D164 "Salaries Held Too Small," *New York Times*, April 19, 1940, Letter to the Editor.

D165 "Interview with Orin E. Dunlop, Jr.," *New York Times*, April 21, 1940, p. 12.

D166 "Obligations of Libraries in a Democracy," *Wilson Library Bulletin*, 14 (April 1940), 560–561.

D167 "The Irresponsibles," *Nation*, 150 (May 18, 1940), 618–623.

D168 "Post-war Writers and Pre-war Readers," *New Republic*, 102 (June 10, 1940), 789–790.

D169 "The Librarian and the Democratic Process," *A L A Bulletin*, 34 (June 1940), 385–388, 421.

D170 "Of the Librarian's Profession," *Atlantic*, 165 (June 1940), 786–790.

D171 "Comments on the Film *The Ramparts We Watch*," *Time*, 36 (August 26, 1940), 42–43.

D172 "Speech on U. S. Democracy, International Student Service," *New York Times*, September 11, 1940, p. 10.

D173 "Speech on National Unity, New York Herald Tribune Forum," *New York Times*, October 24, 1940, VIII, p. 3.

D174 "Impact of War," *New York Times Magazine*, November 24, 1940, pp. 14–15.

D175 "We Will Be Great: The part to be played by artists and writers in mobilization of national resources for defense," *Sphere*, 26 (December 1940), 7–10.

1941

D176 "Speech on Combating Intolerance, Christians and Jews Conference," *New York Times*, January 23, 1941, p. 23.

D177 "The American Cause," *Survey Graphic*, 30 (January 1941), 21–23. Reprinted in *A Time to Act*, pp. 103–116.

D178 "The Next Harvard, As Seen by Archibald MacLeish," *Atlantic*, 167 (May 1941), 582–593.

D179 "New Land, New World," *Common Ground*, 1 (Summer, 1941), 3–7.

D180 "To the Class of '41," *Nation*, 152 (June 21, 1941), 717–720. Reprinted in *A Time to Act*, pp. 67–82.

D181 "We Have no Troth With Destiny," *Sphere*, 28 (July 1941), 29–32.

D182 "Destroy Fascism, If You Think of the Future," *New York Times*, September 11, 1941, p. 6.

D183 "The American Writers and the New World," *Yale Review*, 31 (September 1941), 61–77. Reprinted as "The Problem of the New World" in *A Time to Act*, pp. 43–66.

D184 "The People's Choice," *New Republic*, 105 (October 7, 1941), 544–546.

D185 "Prophets of Doom," *Atlantic*, 168 (October 1941), 477–482.

D186 "Credo," *School Life*, 27 (December 1941), 70.

1942

D187 "Speech on U. S. Unity, National Urban League," *New York Times*, February 12, 1942, p. 12.

D188 "The Library of Congress Protects Its Collections," *A L A bulletin*, 36 (February 1942), 74–75 f.

D189 "A Note on Alexis Saint Leger Leger," *Poetry*, 59 (March 1942), 330–337.

D190 "The Enemy to Be Feared," *Think*, 8 (March 1942), 6, 45.

D191 "Speech on Anti-USSR Sentiment in U.S. at Russian War Relief Luncheon," *New York Times*, April 15, 1942, p. 8.

D192 "Scores Alleged Defeatist Propaganda by U.S. Press," *New York Times*, April 18, 1942, p. 13.

D193 "Enemies of the People," *Life*, 12 (April 20, 1942), 8.

D194 "Books in the War," *A L A bulletin*, 36 (April 1942), 306.

D195 "Psychological Front," *Vital Speeches*, 8 (May 1, 1942), 424–427.

D196 "An Interview with Archibald MacLeish," *New York Times*, May 10, 1942, VI, p. 2.

D197 "Books in Democracy's Arsenal," *Saturday Review of Literature*, 25 (May 25, 1942), 9.

D198 "To Ed Murrow, Reporter," *Journal of Home Economics*, 34 (June 1942), 361.

D199 "Archibald MacLeish Answers 15 Vital Questions," *Look*, 6 (July 14, 1952), 11–13.

D200 "Attack on the Scholar's World," *The Saturday Review of Literature*, 25 (July 18, 1942), 3–6.

D201 "Image of Victory," *Atlantic*, 170 (July 1942), 1–6. Reprinted in *A Time To Act*, pp. 177–194.

D202 "Intellectual Battle," *Vital Speeches*, 8 (August 15, 1942), 665–667.

D203 "New Isolationism," *New York Times Magazine*, August 16, 1942, VII, pp. 8+.

D204 "Geography of This Time," *New Republic*, 107 (October 26, 1942), 542.

D205 "America's Duty to French Culture," *Saturday Review of Literature*, 25 (November 14, 1942), 5–6+.

1943

D206 "Psychological Warfare," *Foreign Notes*, 20 (February 26, 1943), 2–4.

D207 "The Dilemma," *Atlantic*, 171 (February 1943), 37–40.

D208 "Words Are Not Enough," *Nation*, 156 (March 13, 1943), 368–372.

D209 "As We Remember Him," *Saturday Review of Literature*, 26 (March 27, 1943), 7–11.

D210 "Unimagined America," *Atlantic*, 171 (June 1943), 59–63. Reprinted in *Freedom Is the Right to Choose*, pp. 17–29.

D211 "What Will the Decision Be?" *Vital Speeches*, 9 (August 1, 1943), 613–616.

D212 "The Practice of Citizenship," *Common Ground*, 4 (September 1943), 61–66.

D213 "The Fight of Youth," *Rotarian*, 63 (September 1943), 7.

D214 "What Do We Mean by Victory?" *Free World*, 6 (October 1943), 306–311.

D215 "Moral Front," *Nation*, 157 (December 4, 1943), 660–663.

1944

D216 "When We Speak to Each Other of Peace," *Journal of Home Economics*, 35 (March 1944), 146.

D217 "Hope for Every Living Heart," *National Education Association Journal*, 33 (May 1944), 109–110.

D218 "Word and the Fact," *Atlantic*, 174 (July 1944), 52–55.

D219 "Challenge to the American People," *New York Times Magazine*, August 13, 1944, 5ff.

D220 "Memorials Are for Remembrance," *Architectural Forum*, 81 (September 1944), 111–112, 170.

D221 "The People Are Indivisible," *Nation*, 159 (October 28, 1944), 509–512.

D222 "Reorganization of the Library of Congress," *Library Quarterly*, 14 (October 1944), 277–315.

D223 "Humanism and the Belief in Man," *Atlantic*, 174 (November 1944), 72–78. Reprinted in *Freedom is the Right to Choose*, pp. 141–158.

D224 "Hearing of Archibald MacLeish, before the U.S. Congressional Committee on Foreign Relations, to be an Assistant Secretary of State. December 12 & 13, 1944" Washington: 1944, pp. 20–35, 78–86.

D225 "The Frightened Philistines," *New Republic*, 5 (December 18, 1944), 838.

D226 "American Story: Episode Number Ten," *Education*, 65 (December 1944), 218–227.

D227 "The Choice Is Ours," *National Educational Association Journal*, 33 (December 1944), 209.

1945

D228 "Information for People's Peace," *The Department of State Bulletin*, 12 (January 7, 1945), 21.

D229 "Statement by Mr. Archibald MacLeish before the Senate Committee on Foreign Relations," published in *Publishers' Weekly*, 147 (January 13, 1945), 125.

D230 "Poet Speaks From the Visitors' Gallery," *Saturday Review of Literature*, 28 (January 13, 1945), 18.

D231 "Popular Relations and the Peace," *The Department of State Bulletin*, 12 (January 14, 1945), 47–51.

D232 "Cultural Relations," *Vital Speeches*, 11 (February 1, 1945), 242–245.

D233 "The American Certainty," *The Department of State Bulletin*, 12 (February 18, 1945), 238–240.

D234 "People Must Speak to People," *New York Times Magazine*, February 18, 1945, VI, p. 9+.

D235 "World Trade and World Peace," *The Department of State Bulletin*, 12 (March 11, 1945), 401–408. With Dean Acheson, William L. Clayton, and Kennedy Ludlam.

D236 "What About the Liberated Areas?" *The Department of State Bulletin*, 12 (March 18, 1945), 441–448. With James C. Dunn, Charles P. Taft, and Kennedy Ludlam.

D237 "What About the Enemy Countries?" *The Department of State Bulletin*, 12 (March 25, 1945), 480–486. With James C. Dunn, Robert Murphy, and Kennedy Ludlam.

D238 "America's Good Neighbours," *The Department of State Bulletin*, 12 (April 1, 1945), 547–554. With Nelson Rockefeller, Avra Warren, Spruille Braden, and Kennedy Ludlam.

D239 "A Means to Peace," *The Department of State Bulletin*, 12 (April 1, 1945), 570.

D240 "It's Your State Department," *The Department of State Bulletin*, 12 (April 8, 1945), 629–637. With Julius C. Holmes, Michael J. McDermott, and Walter Raney.

D241* "We've Been Pretending That We Didn't Know It's Just One World," *San Francisco Chronicle*, April 25, 1945, p. 5.

D242 "United States-Soviet Relations," *The Department of State Bulletin*, 12 (May 27, 1945), 950–952.

D243 "April Elegy: April 15–April 12," *Atlantic*, 175 (June 1945), 43.

D244 "On the Threshold of World Oneness," *Free World*, 10 (July 1945), 13–16.

D245 "The United Nations Charter and Our Foreign Policy," *The Department of State Bulletin*, 13 (August 5, 1945), 181–188. With Dean Acheson.

D246 "Our Relief Policy for Europe," *The Department of State Bulletin*, 13 (August 12, 1945), 242–248. With Joseph C. Grew and Willard Thorp.

D247 "Resignation of Archibald MacLeish as Assistant Secretary of State," *The Department of State Bulletin*, 13 (August 19, 1945), 273.

D248* "Remarks," *United Nations Conference for the Establishment of an Educational, Scientific, and Cultural Organization*, 1 (October 29–November 16, 1945).

D249 "Can We Educate for World Peace?" *The Reviewing Stand*, 6 (December 16, 1945), 3–11. With F. L. Schlagle, Herbert Emmerich, and Francis Bacon.

1946

D250 "Victory Without Peace," *Saturday Review of Literature*, 29 (February 9, 1946), 5–7.

D251 "UNESCO," *Free World*, 11 (February 1946), 19–21.

D252 "The Role of UNESCO in Our Foreign Policy," *The Department of State Bulletin*, 14 (April 14, 1946), 629, 643.

D253 "He Cherished American Culture," *New Republic*, 114 (April 15, 1946), 540–541.

D254 "Museums and the World Peace," *Museum News*, 24 (June 1, 1946), 6–8.

D255 "The Part of Youth," *Atlantic*, 178 (October 1946), 52–55.

D256 "Hope for the World," *New Republic*, 115 (November 4, 1946), 597–599.

D257 "If We Want Peace, This Is the First Job," *New York Times Magazine*, November 17, 1946, pp. 11, 60–61.

1947

D258 "The People's Peace," *Atlantic,* 180 (July 1947), 54–58.

1948

D259 "The Artist as President," *Saturday Review of Literature*, 31 (March 27, 1948), 8–9.

D260 "Last Soldiers of the Revolution," *Life*, 24 (May 31, 1948), 88–90. Reprinted as "Thirteen Candles: One For Every State" in *Freedom Is The Right to Choose*, pp. 3–14.

D261 "A Dangerous Challenge," *Nation*, 167 (July 10, 1948), 29.

D262 "A Progress Report on Atomic Energy," *Life*, 25 (September 27, 1948), 114ff.

D263 "How Can UNESCO Contribute to Peace?" *American Association of University Professors Bulletin*, 34 (September 1948), 539–545.

D264 "Notebooks 1924–1948" [Part I]. *Poetry*, 73 (October 1948), 33–42. Reprinted as "Notes on the Image of Man in These Mornings" in *Freedom Is the Right to Choose*, pp. 33–41.

D265 "Notebooks 1924–1948" [Part II]. *Poetry*, 73 (November 1948), 88–96. Reprinted as "Notes on the Image of Man in These Mornings" in *Freedom Is the Right to Choose*, pp. 33–41.

1949

D266 "Yankee Skipper," *Yale Review*, 38 (June 1949), 610–622. Reprinted as "The Great Grandfather" in *A Continuing Journey*, pp. 343–358.

D267 "The Living Spring," *Saturday Review of Literature*, 32 (July 16, 1949), 8–9. Reprinted as "St. John Perse" in *A Continuing Journey*, pp. 313–317.

D268 "The Conquest of America," *Atlantic*, 184 (August 1949), 17–22. Reprinted in *Freedom Is the Right to Choose*, pp. 79–95.

1950

D269 "The Act of Faith," *Atlantic*, 185 (June 1950), 31–34. Reprinted in *Freedom Is the Right to Choose*, pp. 161-170.

D270 "The United Nations Exists," *United Nations World*, 4 (August 1950), 15–16.

D271 "The American State of Mind," *American Scholar*, 19 (October 1950), 398–408. Reprinted as "The Revulsion of Decency" in *Freedom Is the Right to Choose*, pp. 99–111.

D272 "War or Peace: The Undebated Issue," *Nation*, 171 (December 16, 1950), 595–597.

D273 "Secretary Acheson's Critics," *New York Times*, December 20, 1950, p. 30.

1951

D274 "The Dialectic of Freedom," *A D A World*, (February 1951), 7f. Reprinted as "The Sense of American Purpose" in *Freedom Is the Right to Choose*, pp. 115–123.

D275 "The Power of Choice," *Atlantic*, 188 (August 1951), 41–44. Reprinted in *Freedom Is the Right to Choose*, pp. 127–137.

D276 "Faulkner and the Responsibility of the Artist," *The Harvard Advocate*, (November 1951), pp. 18, 43. Reprinted as "Faulkner at Stockholm" in *A Continuing Journey*, pp. 163–167.

D277 "Presentation to William Faulkner of the Howells Medal," *American Academy of Arts and Letters*. Proceedings. 2nd series, I; 1951. New York. pp. 17–18.

D278 "To Make Men Free," *Atlantic*, 188 (November 1951), 27–30. Reprinted in *Freedom Is the Right to Choose*, pp. 173–182.

1952

D279 "A Chinese Ars Poetica," *Kenyon Review*, 14 (Summer 1952), 524–529.

1953

D280 "Muses' Sterner Laws," *New Republic*, 128 (July 13, 1953), 16–18.

D281 "Loyalty and Freedom," *American Scholar*, 22 (Autumn 1953), 393–398.

1954

D282 "Elmer Davis: Undwindled American," *Nation*, 178 (March 6, 1954), 202. Reprinted in *A Continuing Journey*, pp. 296-298.

D283 "The Love of This Land," *Colorado Quarterly*, 3 (Summer 1954), 5–13.

1955

D284 "The Poet as Playwright," *Atlantic*, 195 (February 1955), 49–52.

D285 "The Proper Pose of Poetry," *Saturday Review*, 38 (March 5, 1955), 11ff.

D286 "Alternative," *Yale Review*, 44 (June 1955), 481–496. Reprinted in *A Continuing Journey*, pp. 148–162.

D287 "Why Can't They Say What They Mean?" *Michigan Alumnus Quarterly Review*, 61 (Summer 1955), 291–301. Reprinted in *A Continuing Journey*, pp. 188–209.

1956

D288 "Why Do We Teach Poetry?" *Atlantic*, 97 (March 1956), 48–53. Reprinted in *A Continuing Journey*, pp. 213–226.

D289, "Changes in the Weather," *New Republic*, 135 (July 2, 1956), 16–19. Reprinted in *A Continuing Journey*, pp. 49–58.

D290 "The Prologue to *J.B.*," *Saturday Review*, 39 (September 1, 1956), 7–10.

D291 "A Clean Politics Appeal," *Harper's Magazine*, 213 (October 1956), 97.

D292 "A Dedication," *Carleton College Bulletin*, 53 (November 1956), 1–14. Reprinted in *A Continuing Journey*, pp. 115–129.

D293 "Library Buildings, Whys and Wherefores," *Library Journal*, 81 (December 1, 1956), 27–38.

D294 "In Praise of Dissent," *New York Times Book Review*, December 16, 1956, p. 5.

1957

D295 "The Poet and America," *Carolina Quarterly*, 9 (Winter 1957), 5–13.

D296 "Readers to Readers: A Parenthesis," *Botteghe Oscure*, 20 (1957), 11–15.

1958

D297 "Isolation of the American Artist," *Atlantic*, 201 (January 1958), 55–59. Reprinted in *A Continuing Journey*, pp. 176–187.

D298 "Interview with Jean White," *Washington Post and Times Herald*, November 30, 1958, Section D, p. 13.

D299 "About a Trespass on a Monument," *The New York Times*, December 7, 1958, II, 5+.

1959

D300 "What Is a True University?" *Saturday Review*, 42 (January 31, 1959), 11–13.

D301 "Poet and the Press," *Atlantic*, 203 (March 1959), 40–46.

D302 "The Book of Job," *Christian Century*, 76 (April 8, 1959), 419–422.

D303 "The Men Behind *J.B.*" *Theater Arts*, 43 (April 1959), 60–63.

D304 "The Staging of a Play," *Esquire*, 51 (May 1959), 144–158.

D305 "On the Teaching of Writing," *Harper's*, 219 (October 1959), 158–161. Reprinted in *A Continuing Journey*, pp. 227–233.

D306 "The Final Disaster," *Senior Scholastic*, 75 (November 4, 1959), 14.

1960

D307 "Archibald MacLeish: On Being a Poet in the Theater" [interview], *Horizon*, 2 (January 1960), 48–56.

D308 "*J.B.*," *Theater Arts*, 44 (February 1960), 36–44.

D309 "We Have Purpose, We All Know It," *Life*, 48 (May 30, 1960), 86. Reprinted as "National Purpose" in *A Continuing Journey*, pp. 77–86.

D310 "Requiem for a Literary Haven," *Saturday Review*, 43 (November 26, 1960), 26, 39.

D311 "To Face the Real Crisis: Man Himself," *New York Times Magazine*, December 25, 1960, pp. 5, 29–30.

1961

D312 "Jorge Guillen," *Atlantic*, 207 (January 1961), 127–128. Reprinted in *A Continuing Journey*, pp. 333–336.

D313 "Jane Addams and the Future," *Social Service Review*, 35 (March 1961), 1–5.

D314 "His Mirror Was Danger," *Life*, 51 (July 14, 1961),
71–73. Reprinted as "Ernest Hemingway" in *A Continuing
Journey*, pp. 307–312. Translated into Spanish in *Life,
en Español*, 18 (August 7, 1961), 23–24.

D315 "Our Lives, Our Fortunes, and Our Sacred Honor,"
Think, 27 (July/August 1961), 2–23.

D316 "Antidotes for Twitching: Exerpts from Poetry and
Experience," *Saturday Review*, 44 (August 12, 1961), 24.

D317 "What Is English," *Saturday Review*, 44 (December 9,
1961), 12–14.

1962

D318 "Eleanor Roosevelt 1884–1962," *Nation*, 195
(November 17, 1962), 317. Reprinted in *A Continuing
Journey*, pp. 277–280.

1963

D319 "A Retiring View of Harvard," *Harvard Alumni
Bulletin*, (January 12, 1963), 309–311. Reprinted in *A
Continuing Journey*, pp. 260–265.

D320 "Must We Hate," *Atlantic*, 211 (February 1963), 79–82.
Reprinted as "A View of Oxford, Mississippi" in *A
Continuing Journey*, pp. 95–103.

D321 "Tribute to a Great Lady," *New York Times Magazine*,
November 3, 1963, p. 17.

1964

D322 "Gift Outright," *Atlantic*, 213 (February 1964), 50–52.
Reprinted as "Robert Frost and John F. Kennedy," in *A
Continuing Journey*, pp. 299–306.

D323 "What Has Hatred to Do with a University," *Pelican Annual*, (1964), 5–7. Graduation address: University College of the West Indies.

1965

D324 "The Eleanor Roosevelt Story," *McCalls*, 92 (May 1965), 98ff.

D325 "What Is Realism Doing to American History," *Saturday Review*, 48 (July 3, 1965), 10–12. Reprinted as "A Decent Respect" in *A Continuing Journey*, pp. 104–114.

D326 "Former Librarian of Congress Questions U. S. Foreign Policy," *Library Journal*, 90 (July 1965), 2984.

D327 "U. N. Holds Memorial Service for Ambassador Stevenson," *The Department of State Bulletin*, 53 (August 9, 1965), 231–233.

D328 "A Talent for Joy," *Saturday Review*, 48 (November 29, 1965), 25–26. Reprinted as "F.F." in *A Continuing Journey*, pp. 286–291.

1966

D329 "There Was Something About the Twenties," *Saturday Review*, 49 (December 31, 1966), 10–13. Sections reprinted in "Who Precisely Do You Think You Are" in *A Continuing Journey*, pp. 3–11.

D330 "Felix Frankfurter: A Lesson of Faith," *Supreme Court Review* (1966), 1–5.

1967

D331 "The Seat Behind the Pillar," *New York Times*, January 21, 1967, p. 30.

D332 "Thoughts on an Age That Gave Us Hiroshima," *New York Times*, July 9, 1967, p. 1.

D333 "When We Are Gods," *Saturday Review*, 50 (October 14, 1967), 22.

D334 "Magic Prison," *Saturday Review*, 50 (October 28, 1967), 21–23.

1968

D335 "The Great American Frustration," *Saturday Review*, 51 (July 13, 1968), 13–16.

D336 "Changes in the Ritual of Library Dedication: The Dedication of a Library in the McCarthy Era Became 'an Act of War'; Today It Is an Affirmation That 'the Man Comes First, Before the Information,' " *Library Journal*, 93 (October 1, 1968), 3517–3520.

D337 "A Memorial Tribute to Carl Sandburg," *Massachusetts Review*, 9 (Winter 1968), 41–44.

D338 "A Greeting" in A Symposium in Honor of Jorge Guillen at 75, *Books Abroad*, 42 (Winter 1968), 48.

D339 "A Reflection: Riders on Earth Together, Brothers in Eternal Cold," *New York Times*, December 25, 1968, p. 1. Reprinted as "Brothers in the Eternal Cold," *Reader's Digest*, 94 (March 1969), 68–69.

1969

D340 "Revolt of the Diminished Man," *Saturday Review*, 52 (June 7, 1969), 16–19.

D341 "Archibald MacLeish Describes Emily Dickinson Film," *Emily Dickinson Bulletin*, No. 9 (June 1969), 31.

D342 "Festival of Freedom," *Saturday Review*, 53 (August 29, 1970), 16.

D343 "A 7-Year Scratch," *New York Times*, October 25, 1970, II, pp. 1, 22.

D344 "Trustee of the Culture," *Saturday Review*, 53 (December 19, 1970), 18–19.

1971

D345 "Cottonwoods Astir," *Saturday Review*, 54 (November 13, 1971), 40–41.

1972

D346 "Rediscovering the Simple Life," *McCalls*, 99 (April 1972), 79–87.

D347 "What She [Eleanor Roosevelt] Was *Herself*," *New York Times*, May 4, 1972, p. 45.

D348 "MacLeish Mourns Lost Values," *New York Times*, May 7, 1972, p. 79.

D349 "The Premise of Meaning," *American Scholar*, 41 (Summer 1972), 357–362.

II. Works by Others about MacLeish

E. Annotated checklist of selected criticism

The annotations in this checklist indicate at least one direction of thought followed in the work concerned and are not meant to be a definitive summary of the article's contents.

1926

E1 Monroe, Harriet. "Tone Poems." *Poetry*, 28 (April 1926), 44–47.

In *The Happy Marriage and Other Poems* and *The Pot of Earth*, the editor of *Poetry* finds an "unusual instinct for rhythms and tone-values." MacLeish is a "young poet of rare promise and already fine achievement."

E2 Blackmur, R. P. "A Modern Poet in Eden." *Poetry*, 28 (September 1926), 399f.

A review of *Nobodaddy* in which Blackmur feels that MacLeish has not completely exhausted his subject matter.

1927

E3 Aiken, Conrad. "Another Murex." *New Republic*, 49 (February 9, 1927), 337.

Judging by *Streets in the Moon*, and presuming that he can escape from the influences staining his work, MacLeish "might easily become one of the most exciting of contemporary American poets."

E4 Winters, Yvor. "Streets in the Moon." *Poetry*, 29 (February 1927), 279–281.

While containing "a few rather tawdry imitations of Eliot," the book has "a remarkably high percentage of completely and beautifully achieved poems." MacLeish is one of the few poets who can "rightly take a place beside the most distinguished poets of the preceding generation."

1929

E5 North, Jessica. "Poison in the Garden." *Poetry*, 33 (January 1929), 219–222.

The power and beauty with which MacLeish handles *The Hamlet of A. MacLeish* is marred by the presence of Eliot and Pound.

E6 Galantiere, Lewis. "Hamlet for Our Time." *Nation*, 128 (April 17, 1929), 471–472.

The influences which Rimbaud, Pound, Eliot, St. J. Perse have had on MacLeish have not prevented him from being "the finest craftsman in verse now writing in English."

1930

E7 Zabel, Morton D. "The Compromise of A. MacLeish." *Poetry*, 36 (August 1930), 270–275.

In *New Found Land* Zabel finds a "strain of genuine nobility" which MacLeish must retain if he is to fulfill his potential.

1931

E8 Dangerfield, G. "Archibald MacLeish: An Appreciation." *Bookman*, [New York], 72 (January 1931), 493–496.

An evaluation of MacLeish, from the standpoint of language, up to *New Found Land*. Dangerfield looks on MacLeish as one of the few contemporary poets capable of achieving major poetry.

E9 Monroe, Harriet. "Archibald MacLeish." *Poetry*, 38 (June 1931), 150–155.

An introduction to MacLeish which questions his ability to function as interpreter of his age.

E10 Fitts, Dudley. "To Karthage Then I Came." *Hound and Horn*, 4 (July–September 1931), 637–641.

New Found Land "is fresh evidence that the only successful creator of something new is the man who has mastered, and can use, the traditional."

1932

E11 Kirstein, Lincoln. "Arms and Men." *Hound and Horn*, 5 (April–June 1932), 484–492.

An analysis of *Conquistador's* technique and philosophy which shows why MacLeish is one of the "half dozen living poets."

E12 Monroe, Harriet. "The Conqueror." *Poetry*, 40 (July 1932), 216–222.

A review of *Conquistador*, largely from the standpoint of content.

E13 Jerome, V. J. "Escape to the Past." *New Masses*, 8 (July 1932), 26.

Conquistador shows MacLeish to be "representative of the class views of the bourgeois intelligentsia" searching the past for the values it fails to discover in its dying social order.

E14 Schappes, Morris U. "The Direction of A. MacLeish." *Symposium*, 3 (1932), 476–494.

A study of MacLeish's relationship with the world, as shown in both his prose and poetry, at a time when his social consciousness is beginning to become more evident.

1933

E15 Gold, Michael. "Out of the Fascist Unconscious." *New Republic*, 75 (July 26, 1933), 295.

An interesting document. This article begins as a review of *Frescoes for Mr. Rockefeller's City* but quickly develops into a discussion of MacLeish as a fascist writer. Like it or not, MacLeish is being drawn into 'public' life.

E16 Benét, William Rose. "Round About Parnassus." *Saturday Review of Literature*, 10 (July 29, 1933), 21.

A defense of *Frescoes for Mr. Rockefeller's City* against Michael Gold's attack on the volume as fascist.

1934

E17 Walton, Eda Lou. "Archibald MacLeish." *Nation*, 138 (January 10, 1934), 48.

A review of *Poems, 1924–1933*. She believes that, since MacLeish so well expresses the despair of the 'waste land' philosophy, his poetry is not likely to express the next generation as well.

E18 Aiken, Conrad. "Development of a Poet." *New Republic*, 77 (January 17, 1934), 287–288.

A balanced evaluation of MacLeish's poetry which centers on Aiken's frustration that MacLeish is not fulfilling his potential.

E19 Kreymborg, Alfred. "Moon is Dead." *Saturday Review of Literature*, 10 (January 27, 1934), 435.

A review which sees *Poems, 1924–1933* as the closing chapter to the "lost generation" movement. "Perfection has been achieved and now we must start over."

E20 Morrison, Theodore. "Three American Poets." *Atlantic*, 153 (January 1934), 6.

Frescoes for Mr. Rockefeller's City suggests that the poet "has reached a distinct point of development from which he may be expected to make far-reaching advances."

E21 Blackmur, R. P. "Mr. MacLeish's Predicament." *American Mercury*, 31 (April 1934), 507–508.
Reviewing *Poems, 1924–1933*, Blackmur finds MacLeish's substantial defect as a poet to be "excessive seriousness about himself."

E22 Matthiessen, Frances O. "Poems, 1924–1933." *Yale Review*, 23 (Spring 1934), 613–615.
Because of the diversity found in MacLeish's writing, Matthiessen finds his achievement "somewhat puzzling to describe."

E23 Gillmor, Frances. "The Curve of a Continent." *New Mexico Quarterly*, 4 (May 1934), 114–122.
A survey of MacLeish's interest in the theme of the American march westward.

E24 Warren, Robert Penn. "Twelve Poets." *American Review*, 3 (May 1934), 212–218.
An analysis of MacLeish's lyrical ability based on the evidence of *Poems, 1924–1933*.

E25 Morrison, Theodore. "Three American Poets." *Atlantic*, 153 (June 1934), 12–13.
Poems, 1924–1933 shows MacLeish to be "the most magical of contemporary poets."

E26 Zabel, Morton D. "Cinema of Hamlet." *Poetry* 44 (June 1934), 150–159.
Zabel discusses the relationship of MacLeish's European background to his success or failure as a poet.

E27 MacMullin, Hugh M. "Escape to the Earth." *Southwest Review*, 19 (Winter 1934), 2f.
Poems, 1924–1933 "contains work of a quality rarely equalled in our time."

1935

E28 Redman, Ben Ray. "Panic." *Saturday Review of Literature,* 11 (March 16, 1935), 550–551.

In *Panic,* MacLeish refuses to take sides in the class struggle, but rather concentrates on his role as artist.

E29 Cowley, Malcolm. "Men and Ghosts." *New Republic,* (March 27, 1935), 190–191.

While *Panic* brings a "new intelligence to the theatre," its main weakness is "its failure to visualize or humanize the people who surround McGafferty."

E30 Krutch, Joseph Wood. "Mans Fate." *Nation,* 140 (March 27, 1935), 369–370.

A review of *Panic* in which Krutch says that MacLeish has remained more of a poet than a teacher, and that intellectuals are still unable to tell whether he is with them or against them.

E31 Anonymous. *The Living Age,* 348 (March 1935), 87–88.

A review of the opening night of *Union Pacific* in Philadelphia which concentrates on the American roots of the ballet.

E32 Jerome, V. J. "Archibald MacLeish's Panic." *New Masses,* April 2, 1935, pp. 43–44.

A speech given as part of a symposium following the final performance of *Panic.* This play, by "America's most splendid singer," shows that MacLeish plans to "sing the epic of the proletariat advancing through day to day struggle to power."

E33 Blake, Howard. "Thoughts on Modern Poetry." *Sewanee Review,* 43 (April 1935), 187–196.

A comparative study of Eliot, MacLeish, Stevens, and Crane.

E34 Anonymous. "Broadway in Review." *Theatre Arts,* 19 (May 1935), 325–327.

A review of *Panic* against the background of the actual production.

E35 Jones, Llewellyn. "Archibald MacLeish: A Modern
Metaphysical." *English Journal*, 24 (June 1935), 441–451.
A general survey of MacLeish's poetry touching on both style and
content.

E36 Morgan, C. "The Poet in the Theatre." *Yale Review*, 24
(Summer 1935), 839–841.
A review of *Panic* as an experiment in bringing poetry to the
theatre.

E37 Deutsch, Babette. *This Modern Poetry*. New York: W. W.
Norton, 1935, pp. 214–221.
A survey of MacLeish's themes to 1935.

1936

E38 Aiken, W. E. "Poetic Form in Conquistador." *Modern
Language Notes*, 51 (February 1936), 107–109.
Aiken illustrates *Conquistador*'s indebtedness to Old English verse.

E39 Sitwell, Edith. "Four New Poets." *London Mercury*, 33
February 1936), 383–390.
Interesting for its facile sarcasm, this criticism takes the stand that
in MacLeish "the great British Public have been sold another pup"
for their "already considerably overcrowded kennel."

E40 Cowley, Malcolm. "Public Speakers." *New Republic*, 86
(April 1, 1936), 226.
In *Public Speech* MacLeish has solved the "problem of writing
political verse that will appeal to readers whose tastes have
been formed by Baudelaire, Eliot, and the other great poets of the
Symbolist tradition."

E41 Rice, Philip B. "Public Speech." *Nation*, 142 (April 22,
1936), 522.
The fact that in *Public Speech* MacLeish expresses varying
convictions is not as important as the fact that he expresses any at
all.

E42 Stone, Geoffrey. "Night is Sick with Our Dreams." *American Review*, 7 (April 1936), 98–101.
With *Public Speech*, and despite his movement to the left, MacLeish has shown that he remains one of America's most skillful poets.

E43 Davidson, E. "A Poet Speaks." *Yale Review*. 25 (Summer 1936), 849–850.
A review of *Public Speech* ending with the idea that "the poems ought to confuse no one but the critics who have called Mr. MacLeish a fascist."

E44 Gregory, Horace. "Poets in the Theatre." *Poetry*, 48 (July 1936), 224–225.
Gregory questions both MacLeish's technical proficiency and purpose in *Panic*.

E45 Tate, Allen. *Reactionary Essays on Poetry and Ideas*. New York: Scribner, 1936, pp. 202–209.
A study of *Conquistador* from the viewpoints of meaning and form.

1937

E46 Dukes, Ashley. "The English Scene." *Theatre Arts*, 21 (February 1937), 105.
This article includes a brief discussion of *Panic*'s structural weaknesses, yet evaluates it as "the most vivid modern verse-play that has yet appeared."

E47 Cowley, Malcolm. "Muse at the Microphone." *New Republic*, 91 (May 26, 1937), 78.
MacLeish has not been entirely successful in transforming private speech into public speech in *The Fall of the City*.

E48 Seldes, G. "The People and the Arts." *Scribner's Monthly*, 101 (June 1937), 61–62.
The Fall of the City is so important "as to make everything else in the field comparatively negligible."

E49 Wade, Mason. "The Anabasis of A. MacLeish." *North American Review*, 243 (Summer 1937), 330–343.
A description of MacLeish's intellectual anabasis through the twenties and thirties.

E50 Wyatt, Euphemia. "Post-war Poets and the Theatre." *Catholic World*, 145 (August 1937), 600.
A general review of the subject which deals briefly with *The Fall of the City*.

E51 Quinn, Kerker. "Poets into Playwrights." *Virginia Quarterly Review*, 13 (Autumn 1937), 616–620.
A study of *The Fall of the City* and *The Ascent of F6* against a background of traditional verse drama.

1938

E52 Eaton, Walter P. "Mr. MacLeish, Lecturer." [*sic*] *Commonweal*, 27 (March 25, 1938), 602–603.
Discussion of the concept of the private voice and the public voice in poetry, based on a lecture given by MacLeish.

E53 Lorentz, Pare. "We Don't Know . . ." *Saturday Review of Literature*, 17 (April 2, 1938), 6.
The photographs of *Land of the Free* succeed in putting into words the sorrow and dignity which MacLeish's poetry fails to communicate.

E54 Walton, Eda L. "Land of the Free." *Nation*, 146 (April 2, 1938), 390.
MacLeish's poem serves as a "sound track" for the photographs.

E55 Morrison, Charles C. "Land of the Free." *Christian Century*, 55 (April 13, 1938), 455–456.
MacLeish's 200–300 line commentary is "poignant and piercing."

E56 Denison, Merrill. "Radio and the Writer." *Theatre Arts*, 22 (May 1938), 366–369.

The Fall of the City marked radio's "first use as a medium for serious creative expression by an American writer of major calibre."

E57 Deutsch, Babette. "Meaning and Being." *Poetry*, 52 (June 1938), 153–156.

Deutsch feels that, in *Land of the Free*, MacLeish is willing to sidestep his role as poet and to have the photographs make the public speech.

E58 Schofer, Richard. "Public Thought in Modern Poetry." *Yale Review*, 27 (Summer 1938), 862–864.

A review of MacLeish's earlier *Yale Review* article "Public Speech and Private Speech in Poetry," pointing out that all poetry should be judged by its individual artistry.

E59 Rosenberg, Harold. "The God in the Car." *Poetry*, 52 (September 1938), 334–342.

A rebuttle of MacLeish's "In Challenge Not Defense" (*Poetry*, July 1938) dealing with the role of the poet in the modern world. MacLeish briefly answers Rosenberg in a letter immediately following this September article.

E60 Mizener, Arthur. "The Poetry of Archibald MacLeish." *Sewanee Review*, 46 (October 1938), 501–519.

An analysis of MacLeish's poetic development, emphasizing the various shifts in MacLeish's feelings.

E61 Van Ghent, Dorothy. "The Poetry of Archibald MacLeish." *Science and Society*, 2 (Fall 1938), 500–511.

MacLeish's reality, during the previous twenty years, has changed "from a gilded platonic essence to human creatures and contemporary situations."

E62 Lockridge, R. "Air Raid." *Saturday Review of Literature*, 19 (December 31, 1938), 7.

"Mr. MacLeish, clearly one of our best poets, is not, in *Air Raid*, any closer to the theatre than he was, say, in *Panic*."

E63 Larkin, Oliver. "Air Waves and Sight Lines." *Theatre Arts*, 22 (December 1938), 890–897.

A comparison of the broadcast of *The Fall of the City* and its presentation as a dance drama by Smith College.

1939

E64 Wilson, Edmund. "The Omlet of A. MacLeish." *New Yorker*, 19 (January 14, 1939), 23–24.

One of the most cutting criticisms of MacLeish, this short satire (using MacLeish's voice and even his punctuation) criticizes MacLeish for being immitative in style and superficial in content.

E65 Isaacs, Hermine. "Fall of Another City." *Theatre Arts*, 23 (February 1939), 147–149.

A comparison of the effect of listening to *Air Raid* with the effect of reading the script in book form.

E66 Canby, H. S. "Archibald MacLeish and the Library of Congress." *Saturday Review of Literature*, 20 (June 17, 1939), 8.

Canby defends MacLeish's appointment against those who would have preferred a professional librarian.

E67 Kirchwey, F. "Some personalities of the week." *Nation*, 148 (June 17, 1939) 689.

Praise of the decision to appoint MacLeish as Librarian of Congress.

E68 Chamberlain, John. "Archibald MacLeish." *Saturday Review of Literature*, 20 (June 24, 1939), 10–11.

A defense of MacLeish's appointment as Librarian of Congress on the basis of his personal abilities.

E69 Wheelwright, J. "Toward the Recovery of Speech." *Poetry*, 54 (June 1939), 164–167.

Air Raid is the "soundest" of MacLeish's works.

E70 Raney, M. Llewellyn. "MacLeish's Case." *Library Journal*, 64 (July 1939), 522.

A vote of confidence in MacLeish's appointment as Librarian of Congress, despite contrary sentiments shown by other librarians.

E71 Esdaile, Arundell and Stanley Jast. "Librarian of Congress." *Library Association Record*, 41 (August 1939), 430–431.

Esdaile, despite serious reservations, accepts MacLeish's appointment as Librarian. Jast, expressing a sentiment common to a large number of professional librarians, bemoans the fact that a non-professional has been chosen as librarian.

E72 Kunitz, Stanley J. "Archibald MacLeish, Librarian." *Wilson Library Bulletin*, 14 (September 1939), 57.

Support for MacLeish's appointment and disagreement with the "extremes of indignation and denunciation" voiced by the American Library Association against the appointment.

E73 Paine, Clarence S. "Looking Forward." *Wilson Library Bulletin*, 14 (October 1939), 138–139.

A short reasoned defense of MacLeish as Librarian of Congress.

E74 Kohler, Dayton. "MacLeish and the Modern Temper." *South Atlantic Quarterly*, 38 (October 1939), 416–426.

MacLeish, in his public speech, is the spokesman of the modern age.

E75 Brooks, Cleanth. *Modern Poetry and the Tradition*. University of North Carolina Press, 1939, pp. 110–135.

A study of Frost, MacLeish, and Auden.

1940

E76 Bishop, John Peale. "The Muse at the Microphone."
Nation, 150 (February 3, 1940), 132–133.
Although Bishop praises the verse of *Air Raid*, he does not feel
that the play can be termed tragedy.

E77 Brinnin, John Malcolm. "For a Wider Audience." *Poetry*,
56 (April 1940) 43–46.
MacLeish, in *America Was Promises*, is reworking "in new
combinations, old rhythms and phrases as well as old attitudes."

E78 Melcher, Frederic G. "Counsel for the Situation."
Publishers Weekly, 137 (June 1, 1940), 2125.
An editorial suggesting that the new Librarian of Congress is "a
prophet with a vision and a rare gift of speech."

E79 Wilson, Edmund. "Archibald MacLeish and 'The Word.' "
New Republic, 103 (July 1, 1940), 30–32.
Wilson presents a reasoned response to MacLeish's "Post-war
Writers and Pre-war Readers."

E80 Honig, Edwin. "History, Document, and Archibald
MacLeish." *Sewanee Review*, 48 (July 1940), 385–396.
A study of MacLeish's use of history to confirm the matter of
present perception.

E81 Laski, Harold. "Letter to MacLeish." *New Republic*, 103
(September 2, 1940), 299–300.
Laski suggests that the isolation of the present generation stems
from roots different from those suggested by MacLeish.

E82 Hook S. "Metaphysics, War, and the Intellectuals."
Menorah Journal, 28 (Autumn 1940), 326–337.
A discussion of MacLeish, Mumford, and Frank against the
background of their previous interest in Communism.

E83 Edison, George. "Thematic symbols in the poetry of Aiken and MacLeish." *University of Toronto Quarterly*, 10 (October 1940), 12–26.

A study of nature as symbol in MacLeish and Aiken.

E84 Rascoe, Burton. "Tough-Muscle Boys of Literature." *American Mercury*, 51 (November 1940), 369–374.

A bitter, and somewhat personal, attack on MacLeish for beginning a new trend with *The Irresponsibles*.

E85 Zabel, Morton D. "The Poet on Capital Hill." *Partisan Review*, 8 (January 1941), 2–19. Continued in 8 (March 1941), 128–145.

Quoting from a wide range of MacLeish's writings, Zabel explores the values which MacLeish has propounded during the preceding decades.

E86 Cowley, Malcolm. "Poets and Prophets." *New Republic*, 104 (May 5, 1941), 639–640.

While agreeing basically with MacLeish's position regarding the American situation, Cowley feels that MacLeish "has been exaggerating the political importance of intellectuals in general and poets in particular."

E87 Schriver, Harry C. and Cedric Larson. "Archibald MacLeish's Two Years as Librarian." *Saturday Review of Literature*, 24 (October 18, 1941), 10–11.

A brief description of the "nearly incredible metamorphosis" undergone by the Library of Congress during MacLeish's first two years as Librarian. This article was revised as "Library of Congress Reorganized" for the *Wilson Library Bulletin*, 16 (February 1942), 460–464.

E88 Loveman, Amy. "A Poet in Government." *Saturday Review of Literature*, 24 (November 1, 1941), 10.

Approval of MacLeish as director of the Office of Facts and Figures, tempered with regret that MacLeish will be temporarily lost to the world of literature.

E89 Brenner, Rica. *Poets of Our Time.* New York: Harcourt, Brace and Company, 1941, pp. 45–104.

A long study of MacLeish's writings and ideas, containing useful biographical information as well.

E90 Cargill, Oscar. *Intellectual America.* New York: MacMillan, 1941, pp. 281–292.

Cargill traces MacLeish from the decadent twenties through to the early forties.

1942

E91 Baum, Maurice. "Scholar, Scholarship, and the War." *Vital Speeches,* 8 (July 1, 1942), 563–565.

A speech given at Kent State University, May 19, 1942, in which Maurice Baum comes to grips with MacLeish's concept of scholars as "irresponsibles."

E92 Gillis, James M. "Immune to History." *Catholic World,* 156 (October 1942), 1–5.

An editorial comment on a speech, "The New Isolationism," given by MacLeish at Cambridge University.

1943

E93 Jarrell, Randall. "The Fall of the City." *Sewanee Review,* 51 (April 1943), 267–280.

MacLeish, who is "an extraordinary case of arrested development," has written a "schematized, arbitrarily one-sided, and melodramatic oversimplification" of reality.

E94 Sanders, Gerald. "Pony Rock." *Explicator,* 2 (October 1943), no. 8.

A partial explication of the poem, though Sanders explains neither the title nor the identity of H.T.C.

E95 Sickles, Eleanor M. "Archibald MacLeish and American Democracy." *American Literature*, 15 (1943), 223–237.
A strong defense of MacLeish's philosophical coherence based on "his belief in the dignity of the individual, the reality of non-material values, and the importance of the integrity of words."

E96 Waggoner, Hyatt H. "Archibald MacLeish and the Aspect of Eternity." *College English*, 4 (1943), 402–412.
Waggoner discusses MacLeish's search for a definition of man in the human situation.

1944

E97 Orne, Jerrold. "Review of Annual Reports of the Librarian of Congress." *Library Quarterly*, 14 (July 1944), 239–245.
A year by year analysis of MacLeish's reports from 1940 to 1943.

E98 Cousins, Norman. "Down with Poets!" *Saturday Review of Literature*, 27 (December 23, 1944), 12.
A sarcastic editorial aimed at the Senate Foreign Relations Committee for their handling of MacLeish's nomination to the position of public and cultural relations officer of the State Department.

1945

E99 Metcalf, Keyes D. "Merits Respect and Gratitude." *Library Journal*, 70 (March 1, 1945), 213.
Praise for MacLeish's work as Librarian of Congress, and a brief analysis of the significance of his success.

E100 Rosenberger, C. "Poets and Politicians." *Poetry*, 65 (March 1945), 322–327.
A discussion of MacLeish as poet in relation to his appointment to the office of Assistant Secretary of State.

E101 Myhr, Ivar L. ". . . & Forty-Second Street." *Explicator*, 3 (April 1945), no. 47.

An explication linking MacLeish's "talking beast" with the twelfth and thirteenth chapters of *Revelation*.

1946

E102 Gregory, Horace and Marya Zaturenska. *History of American Poetry 1900–1940*. New York: Harcourt, Brace and Company, 1946, pp. 448–457.

A study of MacLeish's poetic development through the thirties.

1948

E103 Amacher, Richard E. "MacLeish's 'L'an Trentiesme de Mon Eage.' " *Explicator*, 6 (April 1948), no. 42.

The poem shows that life's significance is no longer found in the stars but, more simply, in the minute facets of experience.

E104 Rodman, S. "Twixt Pundit and Poet." *Saturday Review of Literature*, 31 (August 14, 1948), 29+.

In *Actfive and Other Poems* MacLeish is still caught between his two roles of public and personal poet. His chief success is in the more personal lyrics.

1949

E105 Carruth, Hayden. "Actfive and Other Poems." *Poetry*, 73 (February 1949), 287–289.

"Actfive," in particular, is a failure because MacLeish is more concerned with his "message" than his role as poet.

1950

E106 Southworth, James Granville. *Some Modern American Poets*. New York: MacMillan, 1950, pp. 122–134.

A general survey of MacLeish's work up to World War II.

E107 Waggoner, Hyatt H. *Heel of Elohim*. Norman: University of Oklahoma Press, 1950, pp. 133–154.

MacLeish's best poetry was written by the early thirties. When the poet began to search for the image of his belief his poetry weakened.

1951

E108 Anonymous. "Archibald and Archie: A Conversation in MacLeish." *The Protestant*, 8 (January–March 1951), 12–23.

Largely a dialogue in the manner of (and concerned with) MacLeish's *Poetry and Opinion*, this article warns MacLeish that the poet must remain independent of politics and rich men if his vision is to remain unimpaired.

1952

E109 Friar, K. "Poet of Action." *New Republic*, 127 (December 15, 1952), 19–20.

A review of *Collected Poems 1917-1952* which praises MacLeish mainly for his lyrics.

E110 Saloman, I. L. "Peacemaker." *Saturday Review*, 35 (December 27, 1952), 18–19.

Collected Poems 1917–1952 is a major collection from a distinguished poet.

1953

E111 Carruth, H. "MacLeish's Poetry." *Nation*, 176 (January 31, 1953), 103.

A mostly laudatory review of *Collected Poems 1917–1952*.

E112 Kalb, B. "N.B.A. Awards." *Saturday Review*, 36 (February 7, 1953), 21.

A report on the National Book Award ceremony in which MacLeish received an award for *Collected Poems 1917–1952*.

E113 Ciardi, John. "The Poetry of Archibald MacLeish."
Atlantic, 191 (May 1953), 67–68.

An analysis of MacLeish's success as a 'personal' poet, based
largely on his poetic line. MacLeish tends to fail when he attempts
public speech.

E114 Joost, Nicholas. "MacLeish's 'Hypocrite Auteur.' "
Explicator, 11 (May 1953), no. 47.

A rather lengthy explication of the poem in light of its source in
Baudelaire.

E115 Whittemore, Reed. "MacLeish and the Democratic
Pastoral." *Sewanee Review*, 61 (October 1953), 700–709.

Reviewing *Collected Poems 1917–1952*, Whittemore shows the
difficulty of trying to pigeon-hole MacLeish as a poet.

1954

E116 Hewes, Henry. "Happy Poetry." *Saturday Review*, 37
(March 6, 1954), 26.

Hewes sees "This Music Crept by Me Upon the Waters" as
possibly the third act of a play, and feels that the script contains
both MacLeish at "his lyrical best" and a great deal of "chit-chat."

E117 Marcus, S. "Power of the Audience." *Commentary*, 18
(August 1954), 172–175.

While "This Music Crept by Me Upon the Waters" has good
qualities, the ironic ending is "entirely unconvincing."

E118 Hay, S. H. "Fall to Divinity." *Saturday Review*, 37
(December 4, 1954), 28.

A review of *Songs for Eve* which briefly shows the relationship of
the title poem to the other lyrics of the volume.

1955

E119 Palmer, J. E. "Seven Voices, Seven Styles." *Sewanee Review*, 63 (Spring 1955), 294–295.

A review of *Songs For Eve* which says little more than that the collection is "critically all over the place."

E120 Jarrell, Randall. "Recent Poetry." *Yale Review*, 44 (June 1955), 602–603.

Jarrell believes that in *Songs for Eve* MacLeish "has made overpowering demands on his own delicate lyric talent."

E121 Bogan, Louise. *Selected Criticism: Prose, Poetry*. New York: Noonday, 1955, pp. 171–174.

In reviewing *America Was Promises* in 1939, Louise Bogan felt that the poem was a political poem written by a man who is at his best in private lyrical poetry.

1958

E122 Ciardi, John. "*J.B.* and *Job*." *Saturday Review*, 41 (March 8, 1958), 11f.

J.B. is seen as "a great American poetic drama" largely on the basis of having forged "a true poetic stage line for our times."

E123 Waterman, R. "Biographical Sketch." *Saturday Review*, 41 (March 8, 1958), 12.

A brief biographical sketch accompanying Ciardi's article.

E124 Fenton, Charles A. "Theatre." *Nation*, 186 (May 10, 1958), 425–426.

A favorable report on *J.B.*, based on the Yale production.

E125 Hewes, Henry. "Yes Is for a Very Rich Man." *Saturday Review*, 41 (May 10, 1958), 22.

Viewing the Yale production of *J.B.* as a work in progress, Howes feels that MacLeish's attempt to define modern man's relation to God has been "stillborn." The play lacks depth of characterization.

E126 Krutch, Joseph Wood. "The Universe at Stage Center."
Theatre Arts, 42 (August 1958), 9–11.
A discussion of *J.B.*, in conjunction with the Yale production,
showing that MacLeish was striving (as had O'Neill) to discuss
the relationship of man to the universe.

E127 Eberhart, Richard. "Outer and Inner Verse Drama."
Virginia Quarterly Review, 34 (Autumn 1958), 618–623.
Eberhart discusses *J.B.* as drama of plot and action, and as drama
of language.

E128 Casper, Leonard. "The Godmask of MacLeish." *Drama
Critique*, 1 (November 1958), 11–12.
J.B. is an artificial medium for the message it carries.

E129 Tynan, Kenneth. "The Theatre." *New York*, 34
(December 20, 1958), 66–68.
Criticism of *J.B.* as a play in which MacLeish states the right
problem in the wrong way.

1959

E130 Hewes, Henry. "A Minority Report on *J.B.*" *Saturday
Review*, 42 (January 3, 1959), 22–23.
J.B. adds little to the understanding of modern man's relationship
to God. The quality of the New York production cannot entirely
make up for the lack of effective drama in the script.

E131 Driver, Tom. "Notable, Regrettable." *Christian Century*,
76 (January 7, 1959), 21–22.
Although the New York production was excellent *J.B.* suffers
from "a sort of theological schizophrenia" in its mixture of
theology and humanism.

E132 Terrien, Samuel. "J.B. and Job." *Christian Century*, 76
(January 7, 1959), 9–11.
"The Character of J.B. is completely foreign to that of the hero
who speaks in the Biblical poem."

E133 Van Dusen, Henry. "Third Thoughts on *J.B.*" *Christian Century*, 76 (January 28, 1959), 106–107.

While recognizing the wide range of response provoked in the critics by *J.B.*, the president of Union Theological Seminary sees it as a "drama of heroic proportions and immense suggestiveness."

E134 Weiner, Herbert. "*Job* on Broadway." *Commentary*, 27 (February 1959), 153–158.

The love theme of *J.B.* is not found in *Job*.

E135 Zigerell, James. "MacLeish's 'Dover Beach'—A Note to That Poem." *Explicator*, 17 (March 1959), no. 38.

An explication showing the relationship between MacLeish's poem and Arnold's.

E136 White, William S. "MacLeish and the Broken Major." *Harpers*, 218 (April 1959), 77–80.

A strong defense of MacLeish and *J.B.* against patronizing amateur critics who would have had MacLeish clear up the whole question of God and justice once and for all.

E137 Hayes, Richard. "The Humanism of Crisis." *Commonweal*, 70 (May 8, 1959), 153–157.

While *J.B.* does not make any fresh observation about the experience of *Job*, it does carry *Job*'s dialectic beyond both tragedy and theology to the safe harbor of "the humanism of crisis."

E138 Niebuhr, Reinhold, Louis Finkelstein, Thurston N. Davis. "Three Opinions on *J.B.*" *Life*, 56 (May 18, 1959), 135–138.

Neibuhr looks upon it as "modern answers to an enigma." Finkelstein considers it as "insight into our deep need." Davis sees it as an "arid repudiation of religion."

E139 Kazan, Elia. "The Staging of a Play." *Esquire*, 51 (May 1969), 144f.

A very interesting exchange of letters, largely between MacLeish and Kazan, as *J.B.* was being readied for Broadway.

E140 Siegel, Ben. "Miracle on Broadway, and the Box-office Magic of the Bible." *Modern Drama*, 2 (May 1959), 45–46.

A somewhat cynical review of the publicity received by *J.B.* at the time of the New York opening, and the play's continuing success.

E141 D'Arcy, Martin C. "*J.B.*, Wrong Answer to the Problem of Evil." *Catholic World*, 190 (November 1959), 81–85.

The problem of evil cannot be solved, as *J.B.* solves it, simply by turning inward. Help and grace must be seen as coming from God.

E142 MacLeish, Andrew. "The Poet's Three Comforters: *J.B.* and the Critics." *Modern Drama*, 2 (December 1959), 224–230.

A discussion of *Job* and *J.B.* against the background of reviews by Tynan, Brustein, and Hewes.

E143 Montgomery, Marion. "On First Looking into Archibald MacLeish's Play in Verse, *J.B.*" *Modern Drama*, 2 (December 1959), 231–242.

A study of *J.B.* from the standpoint of poetic language and rhythms.

E144 Donoghue, Denis. *The Third Voice*. Princeton: Princeton University Press, 1959, pp. 193–212.

A study of the verse drama of Stevens, Eberhart, and MacLeish, using, in part, MacLeish's *This Music Crept by Me on the Water*, and *J.B.*

1960

E145 Ciardi, John. "*J.B.* Revisited." *Saturday Review*, 43 (January 30, 1960), 39f.

Ciardi considers J.B. to be a fatuously self-righteous fathead rather than a tragic figure who eventually arrives at a convincing self-realization.

E146 Fitch, Robert E. "Sickness in an Affluent Society."
Religion in Life, 29 (Autumn 1960), 611–614.

The symbol and spokesman for the American '50's is Job, with his concern for self, rather than the prophets who were more concerned with suffering humanity.

E147 Gassner, John. *Theatre at the Crossroads*. New York: Holt Rinehart & Winston, 1960, pp. 298–305.

A discussion of the Yale and New York productions of *J.B.*, which leads into a wider analysis of the play's merits and defects.

1961

E148 Stock, Ely. "*A Masque of Reason* and *J.B.*" *Modern Drama*, 3 (February 1961), 378–386.

A comparison and contrast of the Job theme in MacLeish and Frost.

E149 Christensen, Parley A. "*J.B.*, the Critics, and Me."
Western Humanities Review, 15 (Spring 1961), 111–126.

An analysis of *J.B.* as a successful tragedy, against a background of critics who do not agree.

E150 Hamilton, Kenneth. "The Patience of *J.B.*" *Dalhousie Review*, 41 (Spring 1961), 32–39.

"The romantic humanism of *J.B.* fails to come to grips with the religious realism of the *Book of Job.*"

E151 Morse, Samuel French. "An Act of Faith."*Poetry*, 99 (December 1961), 191–194.

"*Poetry and Experience* is a disappointing book . . . the poet's interest in 'the means to meaning' which need not be egocentric nor limited to talking shop, has been so greatly generalized in the book that the 'meanings' themselves lack real substance."

E152 Aaron, Daniel. *Writers on the Left*. New York: Harcourt, Brace, and World, 1961, pp. 264–267.

A short discussion of MacLeish's role in the literary wars of the early thirties.

1962

E153 Weals, Gerald C. *American Drama Since World War II.*
New York: Harcourt, Brace and World, 1962,
pp. 182–190.
An analysis, largely, of *J.B.* as a heavily intellectual play.

1963

E154 Grebstein, Sheldon Norman. "*J.B.* and the Problem of
Evil." *University of Kansas City Review*, 29 (June 1963),
253–261.
J.B. as both a religious and a humanistic work.

E155 Sickles, Eleanor M. "Macleish and the Fortunate Fall."
American Literature, 35 (1963), 205–217.
A study of the theme of Paradise lost in MacLeish.

E156 Abel, Lionel. *Metatheatre.* New York: Hill and Wang,
1963, pp. 116–122.
A discussion of what is wrong with Barnes' *The Antiphon* and
MacLeish's *J.B. J.B.* does not add anything new to the *Job* story.

1964

E157 Vann, J. Don. "MacLeish's J.B." *American Notes and
Queries,* 2 (June 1964), 150.
A short analysis of Nickle's view of Zuss in *J.B.*

E158 Bush, Warren V. [editor]. *The Dialogues of Archibald
MacLeish and Mark Van Doren.* New York: Dutton, 1964.
MacLeish and Van Doren cover a wide range of subjects during a
series of conversations taped during one of Van Doren's visits to
MacLeish's home.

1965

E159 Mearns, David C. "Brush of a Comet." *Atlantic*, 215 (May 1965), 90–92.

An assessment of MacLeish as Librarian of Congress, this article includes the correspondence between F.D.R. and Felix Frankfurter on the question of appointing MacLeish.

E160 Falk, Signi Lenea. *Archibald MacLeish*. New York: Twayne, 1965.

The only full-length study of MacLeish, this book is part of the Twayne United States Author Series.

E161 Lewis, Allen. *American Plays and Playwrights of the Contemporary Theatre*. New York: Crown, 1965, pp. 116–125.

The theme of *J.B.* is too heavy for MacLeish to handle without "the depth of insight nor the gift of poetry nor the theatrical magic worthy of his intent."

1967

E162 Eberhart, Richard. "Archibald MacLeish's *Herakles*." *Virgina Quarterly Review*, 43 (Summer 1967), 499–503.

A "play of poetical ideas" rather than a "full-bodied" play, the book "presents a splendid new creation in American verse drama, splendid, swift, passionate, and just."

E163 Wain, John. "Mr. MacLeish's New Play." *New Republic*, 157 (July 22, 1967), 25+.

After joining MacLeish with Yeats, Eliot, Thomas, and Cocteau in the use of mythology, Wain considers *Herakles* to be a more successful play than *J.B.* from the standpoint of "being."

E164 Gottesman, Lillian. "The Hamlet of A. MacLeish." *College Language Association Journal*, 11 (December 1967), 157–162.

Rather than looking to MacLeish's earlier poems, Gottesman

attempts to find the significance of MacLeish's *Hamlet* in its Shakespearean ancestor.

E165 Sullivan, Harry R. "MacLeish's Ars Poetica." *English Journal*, 56 (December 1967), 1280–1283.
A straightforward exegesis of "Ars Poetica."

E166 Jaffe, Dan. "Archibald MacLeish: Mapping the Tradition," in *The Thirties: Fiction, Poetry, Drama*, ed. Warren French. Deland, Florida: Everett Edwards, 1967, pp. 141–148.
A study of MacLeish's thought up to World War II.

1968

E167 Hicks, Granville. "Imagination as the End We Seek." *Saturday Review*, 51 (January 27, 1968), 23–24.
A Continuing Journey reflects MacLeish's versatility, his courage, and the rightness of his intentions. At times it also shows MacLeish's inclination toward the large generalization.

E168 Paul, Sherman. "Public Speech." *Nation*, 206 (May 20, 1968), 676–678.
Following his initial praise of *A Continuing Journey*, Paul wishes that MacLeish had used a more personal voice, with less equanimity and a great feeling of personal concern.

E169 Sandeen, Ernest. "This Mortal Story." *Poetry*, 112 (June 1968), 199–201.
Herakles surpasses *J.B.* because MacLeish has not spelled out the spectator's thinking and feeling for him in the process of presenting the tragic oneness of human experience.

E170 Gerstenberger, Donna. "Three Verse Playwrights and the American Fifties." in *Modern American Drama: Essays in Criticism*, ed. William E. Taylor. Deland, Florida: Everett Edwards, 1968, pp. 117–128.

A study of MacLeish's later verse drama against a background of Anderson, Barnes, and Eberhart.

1969

E171 Goldschmidt, Eva. "Archibald MacLeish Librarian of Congress." *College and Research Libraries*, 30 (January 1969), 12–24.

A very detailed study of the background of MacLeish's appointment, his process of reorganization, and his philosophy of librarianship. The footnotes are especially useful to anyone wishing to do further work on this subject.

1971

E172 Gill, Brendan. "Last Rites." *The New Yorker*, 47 (May 15, 1971), 102.

Scratch shows MacLeish's literary powers to be too strong and his dramatic action too weak to please the audience during the play's four night run.

E173 Hewes, Henry. "Hope Springs Eternal." *Saturday Review*, 54 (May 29, 1971), 55.

Hewes concludes his short review by observing that *Scratch* is "too arbitrary for a drama, too ambiguous for a history, and too shallow for a biography.

E174 Smith, Grover. *Archibald MacLeish*. Minneapolis: University of Minnesota Press, 1971. 48 pp.

While concentrating largely on the poet's lyrics and spending little time on the plays, this American Writers pamphlet quickly surveys the width of MacLeish's career and attempts to indicate his position in the stream of twentieth-century literature.

1972

E175 Campbell, Shannon O. *"The Book of Job* and MacLeish's
J.B.: A Cultural Comparison." *English Journal*, 61 (May
1972), 653–657.
The two works deal with the same basic themes, and the two
figures are "closely paralleled heroes" shaped by the traditions and
values of their own times.

E176 Hallman, Ruth D. "Teaching *Job* and *J.B.*" *English
Journal* 61 (May, 1972), 658–662.
Possible points of departure for teachers doing a comparative
study of these works in the classroom.

Index